OTTO RANK

A Rediscovered Legacy

ESTHER MENAKER

NEW YORK COLUMBIA UNIVERSITY PRESS

Library of Congress Cataloging in Publication Data

Menaker, Esther.
Otto Rank, a rediscovered legacy.

Bibliography: p.
Includes index.
1. Rank, Otto, 1884–1939.   2. Freud, Sigmund,
1856–1939.   3. Psychoanalysis.   I. Title.
[DNLM: 1.   Psychoanalysis—Biography.
2. Psychoanalysis—History. WZ 100 R198M]
BF173.R36M46   150.19′5′0924   81-15489
ISBN 0-231-05116-6   AACR2

Columbia University Press
New York   Guildford, Surrey

For my late husband, William Menaker,
whose abiding interest in Otto Rank inspired this book
and
to Samuel Broadwin
whose constant encouragement made the realization of
this work possible.

Contents

Preface

Rank's uniqueness as a psychologist and psychoanalyst lies in his erudition and knowledge of culture, which made him constantly aware of the social dimension in human development. At the same time his emphasis on individuation made him the forerunner of ego psychology. He is a humanistic process thinker who advances a concept of social relativism; his concern with the very nature of existence challenges all dogmatic interpretations of the human situation and his belief in man's creative potential profoundly affects his philosophy of life and therapy.

To cite one example: in the introduction to a recent translation of Rank's *The Don Juan Legend,* translator David G. Winter points to Rank's early concern with and understanding of the mother–child relationship at a time when, theoretically and therapeutically, psychoanalysis was in the grip of a patrocentric and phallocentric point of view. The more recent works of Klein, Bowlby, Balint, Fairbairn, and Guntrip—and very currently Kohut, Mahler, and others—emphasize the mother–child relationship's importance to the development of personality. However, Winter does not make clear whether or not these people have been influenced by Rank.

The very fact of this unclarity documents the extent to which Rank's works have remained relatively unknown and points, therefore, to a missing link in the historical chain of the development of theory and practice within the psychoanalytic movement.

It is my wish to place Rank in proper historical perspective, to correct some of the misunderstandings that have surrounded his theories and certain facts of his life, to present the substantive content of his central ideas, and to relate these to the psychosocial evolutionary processes of our time—of which the developments within psychoanalysis are but one example.

I am well aware that my presentation is of necessity an interpretation—a personal statement which reaches beyond reportage. But it would indeed be an injustice to Rank if, in the attempt to present his view of life, my own affirmation of self and of the creative impulse, so central to his theory, were not to become manifest in my own endeavor. I would hope that my interpretation might find favor among those who, viewing cultural history in a broad perspective, are searching in our time of social crises for a deeper understanding of the interplay of the individual will with processes of social change and progress.

The comment that the secrets of nature, as humanity unearths them in the course of the evolution of our scientific endeavors, can never remain the possession of any special group is attributable to Einstein. Implicit in this insight is a profound appreciation of the power of the human striving to master inner as well as outer reality. In the face of this relentless and restless search no individual or group can claim possession of ultimate truth, which is at best an understanding of events as they are colored by the time-space reality of a historical moment.

From the standpoint of history, Rank belongs more to our own time than to the epoch in which he wrote. In many of his works, especially the later ones, he anticipated the social and psychological crisis of our current transition; he foresaw our desperate search for meaning in life—a meaningfulness of which we have been deprived by the loss of faith in religious orthodoxy; he understood the fear of mortality, and the accompanying striving for immortality; he was sensitive to the individual's conflict between the wish to merge with a larger whole, and the need to emerge as a separate person. Above all, he saw that while psychology and psychoanalysis could expand our insights into an understanding of human personality and could contribute to the betterment of its aberrations, it could not provide that central core of meaning and purpose which—especially today—we so avidly seek and without which we cannot live.

Because of his belief in the freedom of the will and the human capacity for psychological growth, Rank had faith in humanity's ability to achieve personal autonomy, to find meaning, and to live productively and creatively. To travel with him along the path of the growth and development of his own insights is to experience a revitalization of one's own belief in these capacities.

Acknowledgments

In the preparation of this book the acumen, understanding, and sensitivity of Vicki Raeburn as editor was particularly helpful. I wish to thank her, Leslie Bialler and the very cooperative staff at Columbia University Press. Thanks are also due to Alfred A. Knopf, Inc. for permission to quote the passage from Thomas Mann's *Joseph the Provider*, and to Margaret Cleary and Alice McLane for the typing of the manuscript.

Chronology

1884	Born April 22, in Vienna.
1903–1905	Rank begins writing of his wishes, ambitions, and thoughts in four Day Books. They are almost the only direct source of biographical material.
1903	Rheumatic fever causes a heart ailment which would ultimately be the cause of his untimely death.
1904	Takes a position in a Vienna machine shop.
1904	Begins educating himself; reads avidly and discovers Freud's writings.
1905	Writes *Der Künstler* (The Artist) and makes Freud's acquaintance. Freud appoints him Secretary of the Psychoanalytic Society and encourages him to go through the Gymnasium and the University and to devote himself to the nonmedical side of psychoanalysis.
1907	*Der Künstler* is published.
1912	Completes Ph.D. at the University of Vienna. Dissertation: *Die Lohengrin Sage*.
1912	Becomes a member of the "Committee," Freud's inner circle.
1914	Call to service in First World War.

1916   Is sent to Poland and edits the *Krakauer Zeitung* for the armed services.

1918   Marries in Poland.

1919   Returns to Vienna.

1920   Begins work with patients. His daughter is born.

1921   Death of his elder brother.

1920–1923   Close friendship with Sandor Ferenczi.

1924   Publishes *Entwicklungsziele der Psychoanalyse* (The Development of Psychoanalysis) with Ferenczi.

1924   Publishes *The Trauma of Birth.*
            Beginning of severance from Freud and the Psychoanalytic movement.
            Beginning of break-up of the "Committee."
            April 27: Rank sails for America.
            Begins to work in New York, analyzing many members of the New York Psychoanalytic Association.
            June 3: First public appearance before the American Psychoanalytic Association in Atlantic City.

1925–1926   Writes and publishes *Tecknik der Psychoanalyse.*

1926   Takes up residence in Paris. Formal severance from psychoanalysis.

1927   Publishes *Grundzüge einer Genetischen Psychologie auf Grund der Psychoanalyse der Ich-Strucktur.* This is the beginning of emphasis on the ego, and of a constructive human psychology.

1926–1934   Productive years in Paris.

1927   Analytic work and lecturing in New York and Philadelphia during some months of the year.

1929   Divides his time between New York and Philadelphia.

1930   Meeting of the International Mental Hygiene Association in Washington D.C. Rank delivers a paper, "The Training of the Will and Emotional Development," which marks the end of his inclusion in the Freudian psychoanalytic group.

1933   Begins to set up a training institute called the Psychological Center in Paris.

1934   Leaves Paris because of world conditions and sets up per-
            manent residence in New York.

1934–1939 Lecturing, writing, seeing patients; a very busy and intense
            schedule. Failing health.

1939   Divorces Beata Rank and marries Estelle Buel, his former
            secretary.

1939   Dies in New York, October 31.

Otto Rank: A Rediscovered Legacy

For what is true is not the truth. Truth is endlessly far and all talk is endless too. It is a pilgrimage into the eternal and looses itself without rest, or at most after a brief pause and an impatient "Right, right," it moves away from every station of the truth, just as the moon moves away from each of her stations in her eternal wanderings.

ONE

—————

Why Rank Now?

TODAY I bought a weapon to kill myself. Afterwards the keen-est lust for life and the greatest courage towards death grew up in me."[1] Thus wrote Rank as a young man of twenty, when desperate loneliness and feelings of worthlessness jousted with an abiding faith in his own unique, creative talents to produce an overwhelming emotional crisis. Contained in this one sentence from Rank's youthful diary is a highly condensed preview of much of the subject matter of his psychology—the role of creativity, the nature of the will, the meaning of birth and separation, the fear of mortality, and the wish for immor-tality. He held the choice of life or death in his own hand and thereby, however unconsciously, perceived the power of his will. Fortunately, he chose life, thus assuming the responsibility for the resolution of his emotional conflict. It was through this very resolution that he became the creator of his own personality and of a psychology of the creative will that has offered us a profound understanding of the human dilemma.

This book will attempt to meet a need and to point a way in relation to the psychology of Otto Rank. The subjective need was expressed to me recently in the words of a younger colleague: "What shall I read of Rank's to get an idea of his thinking?" But even a reading of Rank does not always insure a conscious awareness of his contributions. Anaïs Nin, whose relationship to Rank was close both as his analysand and, for a brief period, as a colleague, said in a talk to the Otto Rank Association in October 1972:

> There are books which we read early in life, which sink into our conscious-
> ness, and seem to disappear without leaving a trace. And then one day we
> find in some summing up of our life and attitudes towards experience, that
> their influence has been enormous. Such a book was *Truth and Reality* by
> Otto Rank, which I read in my early thirties. Its French title was *La Volonté
> du Bonheur* (The Will to Happiness). I read every word and it must have
> penetrated so very deeply to a place where I no longer was consciously
> aware of, into the depths of my subconscious. It was not an intellectual
> experience for me, but a deeply emotional one. So the meaning of this
> book, its guiding principles sank into my unconscious and I did not read
> it again until . . . I rediscovered it and found that my whole life as a woman
> artist had been influenced by it, and proved its wisdom.

Also MacKinnon, in describing his own experimental work on creativity,
was somewhat astounded that in evaluating his data he himself had
forgotten his own early knowledge of Rank's work in this area.

> It was only after all of the data had been collected and I had spent long hours
> pondering their meaning that suddenly I was struck by a congruence be-
> tween what I had actually done in designing the experiment and in selecting
> the samples for study and what I would have done had I recalled at the time
> what Rank had written about the development of creative potential and
> individuality.
>   Since becoming aware of my own strange oversight of Rank, I have
> searched the current extensive psychological literature on creativity without
> finding a single reference to his work. This present neglect of Rank is the
> more striking since it was he among all the early psychoanalysts who was
> most concerned with the problem of creativity.[2]

However, neither the subjective need of an interested reader, nor the
objective need of a psychological investigator can be easily met, for it
is practically impossible to point to a particular work of Rank's that
would meet these needs. Unlike Freud, he did not write any "Intro-
ductory Lectures to Psychoanalysis," nor do any of his works taken
individually give the reader an overview of his penetrating insight into
the nature of man. In fact, the word "overview" is inappropriate, because
it applies to a more or less stable structure which can be "viewed," and
while there are important central concepts in Rank's thinking they cannot

be said to constitute an organized theory. Indeed, Rank was opposed to theory formation in relation to the psychic life of man because it gave the false impression of constancy, whereas the psychic life in actuality is in flux—in a process of continuous change. He regarded the need for a theory about the psychological life as the human longing for something constant to hold onto; to believe in, to give meaning to one's life through an understanding of oneself, and thus to give one a measure of security. At some later point in his thinking he would undoubtedly have regarded the actual structuring of theory as the creative act of a given individual theorizer, reflecting his or her bid for constancy—i.e., for perpetuity, for immortality. But more of this in our subsequent discussion of creativity.

But why Rank at all? He transcended the institutionalization of the psychoanalytic movement of which he was originally a part and developed his thinking independently. The result has been that while in certain quarters he made his mark in a profound way both theoretically and clinically, his influence has of necessity been limited. His psychological writings go back some forty or fifty years. Unknown to the general public, they have been enshrouded by the professional group from which he stemmed in a fog of prejudice, misunderstanding, and ultimately of silence. Ours is not an age to be interested in history for its own sake, nor to understand the relevance of historical perspective for an illumination of the present. "Where do his writings lead?" asked a pragmatic young student, knowing of my interest in Rank. Where indeed? Aside from the fact that all serious thought, to the extent that it stimulates further thought, must ultimately become part of the evolution of understanding, the psychological wisdom of Rank has become outstanding for its timeliness. History has vindicated the promise contained in his views of the human condition. Rank's is an influence not of the past, but one to be felt in the future.

It might be more accurate to say that Rank was so far ahead of his time that our current social turmoil has caught up with a need for his insights. We live in a society committed to change; for example, changing sexual mores, with their emphasis on "freedom and expressiveness," have invalidated repressed sexuality as the principal cause of neurosis and have made apparent the emptiness of simple sexual gratification without a corresponding and meaningful relationship. The need for relatedness, for love, for an ethical interaction among people has become clear. Rank saw early on that humans are ethical animals, by which he meant that our very survival depends on the fact of our relatedness to others and that sexuality is only one dimension of this relatedness. The mother–child relationship, as the matrix from which the ethical dimension derives, was known to Rank long before it became the focus of modern psychological interest. He saw the resolution of the inevitable conflicts this relationship produced as crucial for normal development. His point of departure was the creative impulse in all of life, an impulse that manifested itself in individuation for each living organism—in the human being in the development of individual personality or in an individually created product. Therefore, Rank's nodal psychological point became the mother–child dyad from which the individual must separate and must embark upon a lifelong process of separation, whenever his individuation is threatened.

It is in this view of the dynamics of human psychology as a process oscillating between a striving for individuation and an urge to merge with some larger social entity that Rank is so very modern. For rarely, as has been the case in recent history, has the human creature been more sharply confronted by the need and wish to consolidate a unique identity, and at the same time to become part of some meaningful, communal expression. The awareness of social dynamics as they reflect upon the psychology of the individual, while not new in the history of man's thought, is new and timely in the field of psychology, especially as it derives from psychoanalysis. Rank, with his vast knowledge of mythology, saga, literature, and philosophy, derives his awareness of the influence of social values and mores on the individual from these sources, and is always alert to the conflict between the individual and the collective. In our own times this is a vital issue, since such social factors as, for example, increasing population, rapid communication and transportation, and industrialization, while making for greater interdependence and interaction among peoples, also threaten their longed-for and dearly bought individuality. The conflict between the creation of the self and its submergence in a social whole has become sharper. But it is not only individuals who seek to delineate their individuality; even groups wish to define and differentiate themselves from larger social units. And so we have the burgeoning of national, ethnic, racial, age, and sex groups—

each insisting on its unique character and its specific rights. This is a characteristic aspect of the social ferment in which we find ourselves— a process of psychosocial evolution. Rank was keenly aware of this social process and there is no better illustration of this awareness and of the extent to which he was prophetically in advance of his time than his article on "Feminine Psychology and Masculine Ideology," which we shall discuss in chapter 8.

Rank anticipated the problems that would arise as a result of the weakening of organized religion which had served humans' needs for immortality by supporting faith in the existence of a spiritual dimension in life which manifested itself in the existence of what he called "a soul" (*Seele*). He perceived our need for a belief in the continuity of this soul in some form—a need which could be gratified by identification with a group ideal which transcends the self, thereby conquering our inevitable fear and pain of separateness. The loss of religious faith has resulted in an adherence to secular orthodoxies such as political ideologies and psychological theories.

None, however, have, nor could solve the primary human dilemma— the conflict between the impulse toward emergence, i.e., individuation, and the pull toward embeddedness (to borrow a term from Schachtel).[3] While such ideologies may give meaning to our life for a limited time, they cannot nourish our need for the spiritual nor support our "ancient, illusory belief in the soul," since they are based on a materialistic and "causal" world view, whereas the spiritual derives from "the abstract, the ineffable and the esoteric."[4]

To understand this fundamental aspect of Rank's thinking one must bear in mind his firm belief that we strive to transcend ourselves, to reach for and create even higher levels in the realm of values and thus to perpetuate ourselves beyond our material existence, to immortalize ourselves. We must therefore believe that there exists a spiritual dimension—be it actual or illusory—for it is this belief, this faith, that sustains us and gives meaning to our existence.

While Rank would certainly not deny the proper place of the natural sciences in our striving to understand and master the material world in which we live, he is critical of psychology's attempt to become a natural science and to "explain" human life in purely causal terms. There is a mystery and a never-to-be-explained aspect of our spiritual existence,

upon which our belief in immortality and our commitment to higher
values rests; and it is this belief which is essential for our survival.

Yet, according to Rank, this belief is constantly threatened: from without by the attempt "of legal and social institutions to make the soul
materialistic and concrete," and from within by "the inflated, introspective knowledge of self which modern psychology has established as
a science of understanding the 'causal' motives of thinking, feeling and
action." Psychology is the soul's worst enemy, because in creating its
own consolation for death it becomes compelled by the self-knowledge
it creates to prove that the soul does not exist. Thus it becomes both a
scientific "psychology without a soul" and a kind of overburdening of
the inner spiritual self which, with no support from an inherent belief
in immortality, goes to pieces in a way the neuroses show so well.

In a materialistic age, which suffered from self-awareness and threatened to forfeit its belief not only in immortality but also in religion,
psychoanalysis signified a new attempt to save the spiritual in man, but
it tried to establish this concept in the manner of a natural science. Yet
this kind of realistic psychology could only mean the death of the soul."[5]

Rank's terminology—"soul," "immortality"—could be misleading
if one takes his meaning literally in the concretized sense in which these
concepts are often used in religion and theology. Rank, I believe, refers
to that quality in our psychic lives which is not reducible to material
units and which, in its functioning, expresses the striving to perpetuate
the self by transcending the limits of its material existence and the realities
of the immediate present, either through some creative act, or through
identification with an already communally created *causa sui* project which
becomes our own.[6]

In the struggle to become individuated and to find meaning in the
existence and perpetuation of the self Rank looks to our capacity to will
creatively—to will the creation of our own personalities and of whatever
creative products we are capable, but above all, to voluntarily affirm the
unresolvable conflict-filled nature of life itself through an act of our own
choice—our own willing. Thus, despite Rank's awareness of the importance of the social dimension in our lives, it is for us as individuals
to develop, through the growth of our unique personalities, the capacity
to create our own lives and our own immortality.

This belief in the freedom of the human spirit to make choices through the exercise of will differs radically from Freud's view of man as the product and prisoner of his constitution and of his past experience. Yet Freud's determinism is somewhat leavened by a belief in some flexibility in man's capacity to change the influences of his past. Why else would he have attempted psychotherapy at all? Similarly, Rank does not deny the influence of environment and past experience on the formation of personality. A fundamental difference resides in the concept of change. Since Freud made his discoveries about personality during his attempts to treat neuroses, his model for personality derives from his conception of the effects of imbalances in forces operating within the individual. Therefore, change in personality is precisely that—a rearrangement of entities and forces resulting from therapeutic intervention within the framework of a given structure. Rank, on the other hand, is fundamentally concerned with individuation as a process which begins with separation from the maternal matrix and proceeds through the development of the will to the exercise of choice and finally to the creative act, which includes the creation of personality. Change in personality is therefore the creative choice of the individual's will and must include the assumption of responsibility.

It is in his emphasis on individuation as an expression of the creative life force that Rank most clearly challenges a deterministic point of view in psychology. For not only is each individual psychobiologically unique, and therefore unpredictable in terms of generally applicable laws, but he also possesses the potentiality for further unpredictability through the implementation of this uniqueness in the creation of the new. The capacity for innovation resides in all men, but comes to maximum fruition in the work of the creative genius. Thus the human psyche is governed not solely by principles of strict deterministic causality but also by the unpredictability residing in its creative potential. It is to be understood as an open-ended process in evolutionary movement—a movement that reflects social and cultural factors as well as individual ones.

Rank was departing from the influences of scientific materialism which characterized the scientific and philosophical thinking of the nineteenth century and was himself undoubtedly touched by the same intellectual forces of the early twentieth century which led to the formation of the quantum theory, to the concepts of relativity, and to the principle of indetermininacy in the field of physics.

Lewis Feuer who is concerned with the sociology of the history of science, comments in regard to the generation of physical scientists of the early twentieth century: "A generational cleavage arose in the discussion that was provoked by Heisenberg's principle of indeterminacy."[7] The issue was and is equally divisive in the field of psychology. Feuer goes on:

> Ever since Auguste Comte's time, psychologists and sociologists have been aware that a strict determinist account of human experience was, from an observational standpoint, forever precluded. According to Comte, that was why 'interior observation' had never led to a science of psychology: 'Interior observation gives rise to almost as many divergent opinions as there are individuals believing themselves to be having it.' [in Comte, *Cours de Philosophie Positive* (1830; 5th ed. Paris, 1892), 1:2930.] Comte's argument stated in its generality affirms: Whenever we try to observe our psychological processes as contemporaneously with them as we can, our act of observation alters the magnitude and direction of the observed process; when we try, on the other hand, to observe that process after a time interval has elapsed, that is, in memory, then we find that the dimensions of the immediate qualitative character of the experience can no longer be precisely recaptured. A haze of refractive experiences has intervened. The logic of Comte's argument, as Niels Bohr acknowledged, was exactly that of Heisenberg's principle of indeterminacy.[8]

In other words, the very process of observation distorts the predictability of that which we wish to observe, be it the position of a particle in the physical sciences, or of a psychological event in the human sciences.

However, it is important to bear in mind that the relationship between physics and psychology is indirect; they may both reflect the way of thinking, the intellectual perspective, of a given historical period, but we cannot attribute a causal link to the analogies that exist between them. Human freedom of choice is not contingent upon the existence of uncertainty in the realm of quantum mechanics. Heisenberg himself says: "I do not think that the uncertainty principle has a direct relationship to the concept of liberty. The relation is rather indirect; the introduction of uncertainty into physics has put us on guard against too definite a position."[9]

Rank himself quotes Einstein "under the influence of the facts of atomic physics, contemporary physics earnestly doubts the practicability of a rigid causality." He then continues in his own words: "Near the turn of the century, when this anti-causality movement was beginning in physics, Freud tried to apply the strict determinism of natural science to psychic events, and to demonstrate the principle of causality in mental life from which it previously had been barred."[10] Without conscious knowledge or awareness of the development of a new world view among physicists and philosophers, Rank questioned the causality in Freud's psychological determinism and opposed to it a principle of free will. "I have pursued to its ultimate consequences the principle of causality which Freud applied to psychic events in a naïve 'physical' way, and have been led inexorably to a point where I simply had to derive mental phenomena from a 'causality of willing' in order to understand them. My conception was not that the principle of causality was 'false,' but that it no longer sufficed for our current level of awareness because its psychological meaning had undermined its heuristic value."[11]

The "current level of awareness" which was developing at the turn of the century was an expression of a new phase in man's mental evolution. In relation to the world of nature it manifested itself in new physical theories; in the world of man, in a new dimension in psychology. Freud's orientation with its strict determinism in the name of scientific materialism belongs to the psychology of the nineteenth century. It was a necessary and inevitable step in the understanding of man, for psychology before Freud had but a short history in comparison with other sciences, and had limited its area of endeavor to the observation of surface phenomena, never probing the depths of human motivation. Rank himself, a creative, forward-moving personality, was attracted to the then new dynamic psychology of Freud, but he moved beyond it into the twentieth century. He advanced a relativistic psychology of man in which the uniqueness of each personality conspired with its creative potential to participate in a process of psychosocial evolution that could satisfy the human need for transcending the limitations of the mortal, ephemeral self.

It was inevitable that such a view of man's psychology, guided not by a mechanistically causal theory, but by an awareness of an ongoing interactional process between individual and society and the part played

by the individual creative will in it, would result in a very different
therapeutic approach from that of Freud. Rank saw neurosis "as the
result of an excessive control on the part of the individual's will over his
own nature. In brief, neurosis is the result of willing the spontaneous."[12]

It therefore became essential therapeutically to safeguard the patient's
potential for the spontaneous expression of his unique personality. This
could best be done by an acceptance, on the part of the therapist, of the
patient as "person" regardless of the particular point in emotional development at which he stood at a given time. Such uncritical acceptance
conveys the therapist's belief in the patient's ability to progress beyond
his current neurotic encumbrances. It is the patient's perception of this
acceptance and belief and his/her ability finally to identify with it that
enables him to accept himself in such a way that he need no longer be
overcontrolling, that is, negative and negativistic, but can become positive and creative.

For Rank, then, psychotherapy is a living process of personality development, not a search for an uncertain historical causality, the rational
understanding of which would supposedly result in dispelling neurotic
behavior.

Thus the theme of the creative life process runs like a *Leitmotif* through
all of Rank's thinking: in his philosophy of therapy or his definition of
the will as the force of the ego operating consciously in the exercise of
choice—choice to emerge as a unique and separate individual; in his
understanding of the interaction of the individual and the collective; or
in his penetrating grasp of inevitable guilt inherent in the creative act of
self-delineation.

Rank's psychology—I would prefer to say his view of life and of
man—is a symphony in which the main theme appears and reappears
in many variations. For those who find it difficult to grasp the constant
interaction of the objective with the subjective and whose anxiety leads
them to long for a sharp cleavage between them, the recurrent theme
may appear drearily repetitious. But for those able to eschew the comfort
of objective reality perceived as absolute truth, who can tolerate relativism and indeterminacy, and who can affirm the ongoing movement of
life's symphony, each variation on the theme is both a new discovery
of Rank and an invitation to a further creative discovery of one's own.
It is to such discovery that we propose to commit ourselves in this book.

TWO

Freud and Rank

A Study in Divergent Philosophical Premises

CIRCUMSTANCES are rarely kind to innovators, and it is the fortunate man of genius whose discoveries so perfectly fit the needs of his time and place that they find acceptance in the society of which he is a member. This is probably especially true for those men of genius whose discoveries challenge the established values of a society, be they religious, moral, or aesthetic; for to change values is either to change a world picture, or to modify relationships with others, or to alter one's self-conception. Tradition, that binding element which guarantees social stability, distrusts the new; and men throughout history whose adventurous creativity led them either to explore new territories of the physical world or of the mind, or to find new forms for their artistic creations, have often paid a price in martyrdom, in ostracism, or in neglect.

Otto Rank, who was born in 1884 and died in 1939 at the early age of 55, was such a man. He was a psychologist, social philosopher, writer and therapist. The breadth and depth of his knowledge of culture, acquired initially with little formal education through his own efforts, led him to explore the psychological meaning of myths, the psychology of the creative artist, and the conflict between the individual and the collective life of man. His insights into the ethical and existential problems of mankind are profound, and while his concerns overflow into the fields of philosophy and sociology, he was primarily a psychologist. For some twenty years he was a psychoanalyst and played an important role in the psychoanalytic movement. During those years he was intimately associated with Freud and made significant contributions to the psychoanalytic literature, both to its theory and to an understanding of the therapeutic process.

However, his relationship with Freud ended in a rift which began as a theoretical disagreement, but grew, especially on the part of the psychoanalytic movement, into a vendetta which persists to the present time. To the extent that Rank is known or remembered in the psychoanalytic world of today, except for certain small enclaves, it is as an eccentric and rather insignificant dissenter.[1]

The Freud–Rank relationship has been documented by various authors: Taft, Jones, Progoff. Each writer who concerns himself with Rank seeks out his own special area of interest and makes his own interpretation of Rank's life and work. For Taft he is the disadvantaged young man whose indomitable will, brilliance, and unique creativity made it possible for him to rise above his milieu and to contribute profound insights to the understanding of man; for Progoff, he is a unique genius whose break with Freud resulted in a bitterness, an inner tension and negativism out of which, in opposition to Freud, grew the creative theory of will; for Jones, he is a hard-working, resourceful person of great erudition whom Freud overestimated, who at one time made important contributions to psychoanalysis, but whose mental disintegration—the result of a chronic manic-depressive psychosis (a fortuitous and unfounded diagnosis, malevalently used)—caused great upheaval in the psychoanalytic movement, and was eventually responsible for his own defection. Whatever the emphasis, interpretation or misunderstanding of Rank's personality and of his relationship to Freud, it is important and inevitable for a proper understanding of Rank that we concern ourselves with certain aspects of the relationship between these two great men, since in the contrasting light of their fundamental differences in background, personality, and world view, the subjective derivation and historical meaning of each of their contributions comes into focus.

Psychology, perhaps even more than other fields of creative, scientific endeavor, depends for its insights on the introspection of the investigator.

This is true especially when it goes beyond consciously observable phenomena, when it is more than a study of perception or learning or physiological psychology. The investigator uses himself to understand himself, and such understanding then becomes the basis for observation of others. It is through the interaction of these two processes that he hopes to arrive at some universal truths. But clearly and importantly, the starting point is his own subjective truth.

Freud's psychological discoveries were no exception. They began with himself. He came from a familial milieu which fostered his intellectual and cultural development, perceived his unique capacities, and gave him security and emotional affirmation. He had the personality of a scientist and acquired the educational background which enabled him to pursue the study of some of the most mysterious, unsolved, and challenging problems of the characteristic mental illness of the time—hysteria. As an investigator working within the atmosphere of the mechanistic, rationalistic orientation of the late nineteenth century, he was influenced by its reductionistic and deterministic approach. He concluded that the meaning of the *content* of certain seemingly random psychological phenomena—dreams, parapraxes, daydreams—were not random at all, but determined by factors as yet unknown and unexplored. The concern with the meaning of the content of these phenomena brought insights into the existence of hidden meaning beyond the manifest. Initially these derived from Freud's self-analysis, which grew out of the investigation of his *own* dreams. The subjective experience interacted with his clinical experience with patients to become ultimately a theory of the unconscious which burgeoned into a psychoanalytic theory of personality with a corresponding technique for dealing with its aberrations and malformations. Freud's creative genius gave us a new dimension for understanding the human mind. Things were not always what they seemed to be; and emotions, reactions, and behavior were most frequently determined by forces over which we had little control. That these insights opened up new questions and problems and were not as general nor as all-encompassing as Freud had thought raises issues with which we will concern ourselves later.

Rank was an entirely different personality, and his life confronted him with a completely different task. Out of the creative solution to that task grew his profound understanding of the human dilemma. In fact, his

entire psychology can be derived from his personal growth in the face
of adversity, deprivation, and tragedy. He was aware from an early age,
as Taft has so ably pointed out, of the growth process in human personality.[2] He was therefore less concerned with the meaning of psychic
content and much more with the *processes* by which we become individuated and through which we succeed in productively mastering anxiety,
depression, and the awareness of our mortality. This emphasis on the
growth process addresses itself psychologically to the developmental
aspects of life; philosophically it leaves behind the scientific materialism
and reductionism of the time and replaces it with an existential awareness
of the nature of life itself and of man within its framework; therapeutically
it bespeaks an optimistic belief in the human capacity to effect both inner
and outer change when these are called for by adaptational pressures.

Because the potential for growth is pointed toward the future, it is as
inevitable and irreversible for the psychic life as for the physical.[3] Rank
perceived the need to understand this process within himself as his own
responsibility. At the age of 20, he acted upon this need by beginning
the writing of a daybook. The first entry reveals the purposiveness of
his undertaking and heralds the future psychologist of the creative will:

> Vienna, January 1, 1903
> I begin this book for my own enlightenment. Before everything, I want
> to make progress in psychology. By that I understand not the professional
> definition and explanation of certain technical terms established by a few
> professors, but the comprehensive knowledge of mankind that explains the
> riddles of our thinking, acting, and speaking, and leads back to certain basic
> characteristics. For an approach to this idealistic goal, which only a few
> souls have tried to reach, self-observation is a prime essential and to that
> end I am making these notes. I am attempting in them to fix passing moods,
> impressions, and feelings, to preserve the stripped off layers that I have
> outgrown and in this way to keep a picture of my abandoned way of life,
> whereby if, in reading these notes later on I want to trace the inner con-
> nections and external incidents of my development, I shall have the material
> for it, namely, my overcome attitudes and viewpoints displayed in order
> before me.[4]

Rank speaks of the importance of self-observation in trying to arrive
at a "comprehensive knowledge of mankind" as well as to gain perspective on his own growth processes. There is discernible early in his

writings the awareness of his own uniqueness, of differences from the average man, of himself as an artist, and an "unbreakable faith" in his talents. This faith, despite its interruption by periods of doubt and despair, saw him through many crises in the course of his life and ultimately led him to the profound conclusion that just as he was able to create himself, to be the architect of his own personality, so all human beings have, in some measure, a creative capacity to structure themselves. As we shall see later, this insight penetrated his psychological understanding of mankind as well as his therapeutic procedure. In an autobiographical sketch which forms part of his writings in this early period of the Daybook, Rank speaks of his aloneness, of his emotional isolation, sometimes of his feelings of unworthiness. It would be hard to imagine in a materially limited, yet not desperately poor familial milieu a greater indifference to the needs of a child, or more unawareness of the brilliantly burgeoning mind that hungered for cultural, intellectual, and aesthetic nourishment. It was not to be had in the spiritual poverty of the unhappy home that was his. His alcoholic father alienated both Rank and his brother; his mother saw to the material needs of the family and apparently could give little beyond that in the way of warmth, affection, or understanding to her children. Rank was left to himself and, as he himself rather bitterly says, the only advantage to this method of child-rearing was the independence and self-sufficiency which it engendered.

Nor were his educational opportunities commensurate with his interests and abilities. After completing middle school he went to a technical school which prepared him to work in a machine shop—an occupation for which he was unfitted and which filled him with the greatest loathing and despair.

It was out of this situation that the young Rank turned to books, to the theater, to the world of music. He spent long hours in the library and read avidly in almost every field of thought: philosophy, religion, history, literature, mythology, art, psychology, Darwinian theory. He became familiar with the world of man's cultural achievements. In fact his self-education resulted in so broad, profound, and encyclopedic a fund of information that Ernest Jones, the British psychoanalyst and future biographer of Freud, in the days before Rank's break with the psychoanalytic movement expressed awe in the face of his knowledge. But there was in this activity much more than the acquisition of knowledge, more even than the ability and courage to evaluate critically what he read and experienced,[5] for it was in this period, as he made the acquaintance of Freud's writings, that he wrote *Der Künstler* (The Artist). As Rank himself states in the foreword to a later edition of *Der Künstler*, the inspiration for the work came from reading Freud, especially *Interpretation of Dreams*, and *Three Contributions to the Theory of Sex*.[6] But it is characteristic of Rank, himself the artist, to creatively work over what he has assimilated, to make it his own, to carry the ideas further. He writes in his Daybook, "What another has said never has validity for me until I have experienced it myself; then, however, it has validity only for me."[7] *Der Künstler*, written when he was only 21 years old, is a truly germinal work, for it contains the beginnings of Rank's most significant contributions to an understanding of man and culture.

While at this point, under the influence of Freud, Rank understands the artist's motivation for and production of creative work as stemming from the sublimation of sexual drives, he is already concerned with the social dimension and with the impact of the artist on man's cultural development.[8] The artist's need to gratify repressed sexual instincts through sublimation by offering to society the fruits of his creation speaks to the same need in the population at large. This creation, which is a kind of return of the repressed, influences the culture of his time, which, through the efforts of creative individuals, experiences changes which Rank likens to the rebirth of an individual who, in the course of an analysis, learns to know consciously aspects of his own unconscious. Thus the development of culture is a continuous process, stimulated and given direction by the creativity of exceptional individuals.[9]

It is interesting to note that already in this early work, Rank speaks of religion as mankind's creative attempt to deal with the universal problem of human suffering and conflict. Unlike Freud, for whom religion was an infantile, regressive escape from the "realities" of life, Rank views it positively as a spontaneous mass therapeutic phenomenon which derives inevitably from the nature of man's being in the world. It is the inevitability of human suffering that is important here, for this emphasis on the very nature of life itself, rather than on pathology, permeates all of Rank's later work, and has a profound influence on his view of the therapeutic task.

At the time of its writing, and for many years thereafter, Rank was unaware of the seminal nature of *Der Künstler*, and of its potential for departure from Freudian theory. He thought of it as a contribution to psychoanalytic theory, as did Freud, when the young Rank brought him the manuscript. Many years later, when Rank wrote *Truth and Reality*, he refers to issues which he had already presented in *Der Künstler*, and which had escaped Freud's attention.[10] It was fortunate for both men that the seeds of difference between them were not initially perceived by either one. They needed each other. Freud's acceptance of the work, appreciation of his abilities, and interest in and subsequent generous sponsorship of Rank, opened up a whole new world for the solitary young man. As for Freud, he needed a son to succeed him, to ensure the continuation of his life's work. To my mind, the profundity of this need was an important factor in blinding the great discoverer of the unconscious to fundamental and irreconcilable differences between himself and his would-be adopted son. Both men were creative geniuses who worked over their own experiences, fashioning psychological insights which have advanced our understanding of mankind and therefore, to some extent, have changed our world. Freud, the physician and scientist, began with his own dreams which led to a self-analysis, the results of which he was able to correlate with his clinical observations of patients; Rank, the artist, moved initially by psychoanalytic theory, used the strength of his own purposiveness, the force of his intellect, the determination to rise above his milieu and to structure his own personality, to evolve a theory of the creative will and to relate it to humanity's cultural history. In the realm of psychological understanding, the vehicle is the self.

The characteristics of the historical time and of the setting in which discoveries are made and in which art and literature are created are crucial for an evaluation of their general validity. The importance of the influencing frame of reference in which phenomena occur can scarcely be overestimated. Even in as objective a field as experimental biology, the extrapolation from findings on laboratory animals to general statements about the species under investigation must proceed with caution; laboratory conditions can affect not just the behavior, but even the endocrine function of animals.

Psychoanalysis is no exception. Its theories evolved not only out of the imaginative use of subjective experience by its founder, as we have already described, but also within the context of the culture of turn-of-the century Vienna. Freud was a product of the middle-class sector of that society; the patients who came for treatment and upon whom he made his observations were also middle- or upper-middle class individuals. Initially they were mostly women who suffered from hysterical symptoms. Thus, both in sociological terms and in terms of specific psychopathology, Freud's sample was limited. Yet, from this sample he was able to make discoveries which were previously unknown and to arrive at certain generalizations which seem to have universal validity: for example, that unconscious factors play a large role in human behavior; that dreams are meaningful; that the nature of early childhood experience is crucial to emotional maturation; that in the life of the individual sexual development has a long history which begins in early childhood. Stated in these broad terms, Freud's discoveries have a universality for personality theory that takes them beyond an applicability to a given class or culture. It is when, both in emphasis and specific content, Freud particularizes in the form of the libido theory about the overriding importance of sex as the keystone of all human endeavors, when the castration complex becomes the root of all neuroses, when women are thought to have an inferior superego to men, that the influences of the society in which his discoveries were made make themselves felt. This influence is palpable in the content of what Freud *did* say about the structure and development of personality and the nature of its aberrations, but it is most evident in the things which he omitted. With his strong emphasis on the instinct life as the source of all motivation, Freud came to a concern with ego phenomena very late in the development of psychoanalytic theory and then never from the standpoint of ego as prime mover, or with ego as the executor of will, or with ego as the instrument of creative expression. In these omissions, which define the limits of his theory, we see the influence of the society and the culture in which he lived, reflected both in the nature of the psychiatric problems with which he was presented and in the philosophical world view of the period.

That world view was mechanistic, reductionistic. The cosmos and man within it were thought to be reducible to their primary elements, and the understanding of the interaction and interrelationship between them offered the causal explanation for physical phenomena and for the behavior of human beings as well. It was a Newtonian conception of the universe, which influenced all fields of scientific endeavor and permeated the *Zeitgeist* as it expressed itself in art and literature as well. Relativity, either in its explanation of the physical world, or taken figuratively as an acknowledgement of the importance of a specific reference point in the evaluation of all phenomena, had not yet influenced the scientific and philosophical outlook of the time.

Freud's instinct theory, upon which he based his conception of personality, was grounded in scientific materialism and took as its model the psychophysical theories of Fechner: i.e., that living organisms seek to attain a state of homeostasis and that human behavior is therefore motivated in its desire to reach this state of balance by the need to reduce tension—tension conceived of in the sense of the accumulation of psychic energy, with the corresponding need to discharge it. While there may be situations in which this view of behavior is applicable, it leaves much unexplained. Even more, it creates a specific bias in personality theory and in the therapeutic procedures that derive from it. The philosophical premises which exist most frequently as unacknowledged background for the formation of theory or of creative discovery are never irrelevant for the nature of such discoveries. They express the spirit and thought of the times and therefore operate as social factors which exert an influence on even the most original of thinkers. This theme has been most ably dealt with in Yankelovich and Barrett's *Ego and Instinct*.

The Vienna of Freud's time came under much criticism from creative personalities in many fields who lived in and shared its social climate. It was the time of the twilight and decline of the Austro-Hungarian empire, the end of the reign of the Hapsburgs. Out of the rich soil of its decadence, besides Freud, there arose men like Schnitzler, Zweig, Mahler, Schoenberg, Loos, Kraus, and Wittgenstein. Some, like Schnitzler, mirrored in their work the human problems that the hypocrisy and rigid social mores of the period created; some, like Alfred Loos, the great architect, represented in the simplicity and functionalism of his style a reaction against the bad taste of the period; some, like the writer Karl Kraus, polemicized against and satirized existing society.[11] Kraus was especially critical of the sexual mores of the time; he attacked the moral duplicity inherent in the nature of marriage of that period, which usually amounted to little more than a commercial contract. He saw prostitution as an inevitable outgrowth of the lack of love and gratification in marriage, and defended prostitutes as the victims of this social situation. Ironically, he vehemently attacked psychoanalysis, seeing in it only "its emphasis on adjustment to society" and its threat to the creative impulse and to aesthetic and social values which it sought to explain too exclusively as reaction to the frustration of instinctual impulses. He failed to perceive, for example, that in Freud's discovery that hysterical symptoms are caused by the repression of sexual impulses, there was *implicit* the same social criticism which Kraus himself was making of marriage and sexual duplicity. Freud was not a social reformer; he was almost exclusively concerned with setting up a theory of personality, and with treating the individual patient. But the nature of his discoveries had social implications—in fact, in due time had social consequences. The astute Kraus's failure to see this tells us something of the paradoxical position of psychoanalysis in the Vienna of that time. It was at once revolutionary, challenging existing psychological theories about human nature and existing psychiatric practices, yet conservative in its allegiance to scientific materialism and reductionism and in its failure to take social dimensions into account, or to believe in the possibility of social progress. In this sense it was a psychology of adjustment in which there was little room for the forward leap of human creativity.

It remained for Otto Rank to make this leap, and to explain its nature as a fundamental human characteristic. Rank's interest in psychological issues began with an interest in the creative process as it is manifested in the artist, the hero, and the genius. Early in his life, to which his Daybooks attest, he recognized that creativity resides not only in the originality of the genius's product, but in the life form and personality of the individual as well. The ability to create a life, based on structuring an individual and unique personality, is the outgrowth of the functioning of the human will. In January 1905 he wrote: "Life itself must be formed creatively in and of itself, not confused with an artificial artist life." "If the world is my projection, so is becoming conscious of this projection, my birth. The will expresses itself through the act of becoming born." "Every man of genius . . . is only the symbolic expression of an eternally recurring process."[12]

In these few sentences, written in the aphoristic style in which, in the youthful minds of geniuses, flashing bursts of insight often take form, we see the philosophic premises upon which his later psychology would be built. His thinking is not atomistically and causally oriented, as is Freud's, but holistically and existentially; he is focused on the meaning of life and on man's creative ability to lend it meaning. In other words, his concerns are with being and becoming. His humanistic orientation is revealed in his belief in the motivating force of the human will. In a comment on Freud's theory of dreams entered in his Daybook in December 1904, he wrote, apropos the issue of will: "The dream can only be directed to the fulfillment of *wishes* in the truest sense of the word and cannot fulfill the deepest *striving* of man, nor the core of his highest life; for generally a dream of one short night is sufficient to bring out the desired result, as if the wish were really fulfilled; *to the fulfillment of this highest willing, however, a whole life is always demanded.*"[13] In his intuitive awareness of the movement of human history as an evolutionary phenomenon with its recurrences and changes, Rank could be described in modern terms as a process thinker. To him life was a river; he grasped the meaning of its strong current and the seeming paradox of change within the constancy of its flow. The creative artist, through the constant actualization of his ideal in his creative product, his periodically critical abandonment of his own work to renew the building of his ideal in new form, is the human incarnation of the process of change and flow.[14] These philosophical premises, together with his sensitivity to the social dimension in human life and therefore to the relativity of psychological truth in terms of social change, permeated his later work—to some extent even when he was a disciple of Freud but, most clearly, when he returned to his own, completely independent thinking.

Since philosophical orientation is related to the historical aspects of human cultural development, the contrast in philosophical premises between Freud and Rank leads inevitably to the conclusion that this difference expresses, beyond individual uniqueness, the place in time of each man. Freud comes at the end of an era dominated almost exclusively by scientific determinism; Rank heralds the approaching period of relativism and indeterminacy, when even the exact physical sciences would no longer be committed to strict determinism.[15] In his conception of the problems of human psychology, Rank anticipated the issues of our own time. We no longer live in a time of sexual repression, and of the denial of our creatureliness, which gave rise to the neuroses for which psychoanalytic theory and therapy were appropriate. Having affirmed the body and its urges to a degree that often makes a mockery of the contributions of Freudian psychoanalysis, we have yet to discover and affirm our uniquely human spirit in the exercise of will. Within the framework of a new, freer sexual morality, the inability to love emerges both as the ethical problem of our time, and the source of unhappiness and conflict for the individual. Analysts of a more recent vintage have been aware of this change of emphasis in the nature of human struggle, and, attributing it to social change, have called it variously "alienation" (Fromm) or "identity crisis" (Erickson), or, with a more positive emphasis, striving for "self-actualization" (Maslow). None of them seem aware of any debt to Otto Rank.

The reasons for their ignorance are several, some lying in the history and nature of the psychoanalytic movement, some in the content of its doctrines, and some in the character of Rank, the man, and in the essence of his theory of personality. Among psychologists seeking at times to excuse their lack of familiarity with Rank, it is often said that his style of writing makes it difficult to understand him. While I hold no special brief for his literary mode of expression (although surely he is less obscure, less jargon-ridden, and less turgid than some prominent psychoanalytic writers whose works currently find great favor) I think that the problem lies elsewhere. Rank is an artist. His creative formulations are indeed statements, just as the creation of a melodic theme or of a composition on canvas are personal and universal statements of the artist. But such statements are destined to entice the participation of the viewer or the listener to bring to the experience his own interpretation and to react with his own feelings. Therefore, one experiences a sense of discovery in reading Rank, and each re-reading is a new encounter, since one may come to it with a fresh perspective. Yet there is an unhappy paradox here, for Rank sees man with the eye of an artist, yet writes in a field—psychology—which would hope to be a science. It is not that he is vague, but rather that the scope, richness, and elemental cosmic quality of his perceptions commands the reader's thoughts, rather than offering him answers.

One cannot, in [Rank's] case, as in Freud's, adopt an esoteric and over-simplified terminology to be used in standardized fashion. One must ponder his writings and meanings and selectively incorporate them into one's own thinking and experience. This, in itself, has been a factor making for a more flexible and creative utilization of his views, by contrast to the highly stylized pattern of psychoanalytic doctrine, as was Rank's intention and as he continued to stress in all his later works.[16]

For many readers in the field of psychology accustomed to the structured and systematic theories of psychoanalysis that means a dashing of their expectations.

The situation vis-à-vis the psychoanalytic movement was different. For almost twenty years Rank fulfilled the expectations of the movement and of its founder. Initially, his contributions were devoted largely to the psychoanalytic interpretation of cultural phenomena: myths, literature, artistic creativity, education. It was when he began to do therapeutic work with patients that his clinical observations did not always gibe with the theoretical formulations of the Freudian system of thought.[17] His early interest in creativity reappeared in a concern with individuation, and this in turn led him to speculate about the will, and about inhibitions in willing. From such inhibitions, which he observed in his patients, it was but a short step to the problem of anxiety. Imbued with the habits of historical psychoanalytic thinking, he asked himself: "What is the prototype for anxiety? Is it the response to the memory of some initially experienced anxiety-producing situation?" His answer came in the idea that the birth experience is the first in which the individual, in however dim a way, knows fear.

Rank developed this idea in his book *The Trauma of Birth*. At this time he still thought of himself as an analyst, and had no conscious notion that the book was in any way a threat to psychoanalytic doctrine. Yet it was this publication which changed his life. From the favorite son of the psychoanalytic movement, he became a controversial figure and met its full opposition and consequent ostracism. "Such a recognized interpreter of Freud as O. Fenichel, in his *The Psychoanalytic Theory of Neurosis* (1945) cites Rank's works only up to the time he published his controversial *Trauma of Birth* (1924). Thereafter, presumably, Rank's works, which until then had always been so highly valued, had at once become psychoanalytically irrelevant."[18]

By this time the psychoanalytic movement was acquiring considerable power, certainly within spheres in which it enjoyed recognition. From the time, early in its history, when it was regarded in medical and psychological circles as quackery, orthodox psychoanalysis became by the middle 1920s almost the only respectable psychotherapy. Even the works of Adler and Jung, who by then were well established on their own, were regarded with some suspicion and were characterized respectively as superficial and mystical. Thus the complete ostracism of Rank by the psychoanalysts meant that there was no platform for his voice, no journal for the publication of his ideas; he was not cited, not referred to. As far as the analysts were concerned he might as well not have existed. That he continued to work and write and express his creative ideas is a tribute to the strength of his personality and to his capacity for individual, unique, and separate functioning. His own life exemplified his major theoretical and therapeutic concerns which involved the development of the ability to will independently.

What was it about the *Trauma of Birth* that proved so threatening to psychoanalysis? Taken literally, Rank's theory offered a paradigm for anxiety in human life; he viewed the experience of birth as one which was accompanied by fear—fear generated by the act of physical separation from the mother—and he reasoned that some imprint of this experience remained in the organism. This idea was not inimical to Freudian theory; in fact, Freud himself, in his revision of his theory of anxiety, suggests the prototype of separation from the mother for all future anxiety experience. The nucleus of the Freudian theory of neurosis, namely the castration complex as an outgrowth of Oedipal impulses, is not threatened by the idea of a more primary separation—that of birth which takes precedence over that of castration. However, when the theory leaves the literally physical and seeks to describe *psychological separation*, i.e., *individuation* in the realm of the ego as the core of human conflict, then the cornerstone of Freudian theory, which places conflict in the sphere of the instinctual life, is challenged.

Rank writes in a later work: "This (Freudian) therapeutic ideology rests on the presupposition that man is purely instinctual and that fear is brought in from the outside (hence the concept of castration fear)."[19] Indeed, that the ego itself is created by the impingement of outside influences. Even much later in the history of psychoanalysis, in Hartmann's concepts of conflict-free ego spheres and primary autonomy of the ego, he deals with "ego-instincts" rather than with ego as an original, inherently given capacity.

> The discovery that the freeing or satisfaction of sexuality does not necessarily do away with fear but often even increases it, and the observation that the infant experiences fear at a time when there can be no question of outer threat of any kind, have made the theory of the sexual origin of fear, and its derivation from the outside, untenable. The individual comes to the world with fear and this inner fear exists *independently* of outside threats, whether of a sexual or other nature. . . . Man suffers from a *fundamental dualism*, . . . and not from a conflict created by forces in the environment which might be avoided by a "correct bringing-up," or removed by later re-education (psychoanalysis).
>
> The inner fear, which the child experiences in the birth process . . . has in it already both elements, fear of life and fear of death, since birth on the one hand means the end of life (former life), on the other, carries also the fear of the new life. . . . There is in the individual a primal fear, which manifests itself now as fear of life, another time as fear of death. . . . The fear in birth, which we have designated as fear of life, seems to me actually the fear of having to live as an isolated individual—a fear of separation from the whole—although it may appear later as fear of the loss of this dearly bought individuality, as fear of death, of being dissolved again into the whole. . . . There is included in the fear problem itself a *primary ambivalence* which must be assumed, and not derived through the opposition of life and death instincts.[20]

In these ideas Rank addresses himself to the inevitable suffering implicit in the human condition rather than to a conception of man as suffering from neurosis which can be cured or prevented. He does not deny the existence of neurosis, but does not derive a psychological theory of mankind from its study. His approach is existential. All human beings are confronted with the fear of separation, and with the simultaneous wish for and fear of individuation. The mastery of this fear is made possible through the existence and exercise of will, and in the creative artist the expression of will reaches its apotheosis.[21]

While it was originally the rejection by the psychoanalytic movement which limited Rank's sphere of influence in the psychological and psychotherapeutic world, the failure of these fields of endeavor to show interest in Rank's important subsequent contributions has deeper reasons.

26 *Freud and Rank*

Rank's theories about human emotion, behavior, and conflict offer no organized universal system of thought in which man could "believe." There is nothing of ideology about Rank's contributions, which is in marked contrast to Freud's closed system theory. For Rank truth is not absolute but psychological and relative. He acknowledges as primary and given only the human capacity to structure its own personality through the exercise of the individual creative will. We must look to ourselves for the making of our lives, for the resolution of conflict. Our solace when we face the anxiety of aloneness, of separateness, and the guilt conflict surrounding self-assertion and the exercise of our wills can only be a belief in our own creative capacity. Such a view speaks to our *active responsibility* for ourselves; it offers us no causal, ideological explanation for our normal human dilemmas in the form of early childhood experiences, for example. And since we all feel more secure when convinced that certain causal explanations for conflict or unhappiness are valid, and since we generally prefer to project blame and responsibility upon outer circumstances or other individuals—especially when such projections can be rationalized as legitimate scientific causes—Rank's insistence on individual responsibility would not be likely to find general acceptance.

In working with patients psychoanalytically one encounters repeatedly a fundamentally passive stance, generally unconscious and implicit, but shared by patient and analyst alike: they both believe that the uncovering of the repressed unconscious impulses together with the cause for the repression, and the interpretation of these will effect the cure. True, analysts speak of the fact that through the lifting of repressions, or the analysis of defenses generally, the ego is freed to make new choices in adapting to reality; but in this very formulation the ego is "acted upon" rather than "acting" in Rank's primary sense of willing. This points up a basic philosophic difference between Freudian and Rankian psychology which is crucial for the theory and therapy of personality. The former is materialistic, reductionistic, and deterministic. Personality structure as well as its anomalies are seen as reducible to causal factors over which the individual has but limited control. In the Rankian view the specifically human attribute is individual variability in the functioning of ego which allows for the creation of new and unpredictable factors both within the personality and in the outer world. Therefore, no universal system of causality is applicable to the understanding of the psychological. Personality changes which occur in life, and as a result of psychotherapy, derive from a new experience in relationship, and not solely from an interpretation of causal connections. The responsibility for affirming experience—that is, for overcoming the fear of living—falls upon the individual and cannot be circumvented by adopting a system of explanations as a justification for one's individual plight.

It is not hard to imagine that during a period in which the rationalistic, "scientific," world view, and a parallel view of personality predominated, Rank's view would inevitably have met with considerable resistance. This is an important reason for his obscurity and for the fact that it was possible for the psychoanalytic movement to silence him.

However, times have changed. In a setting of drastic social change, of disillusionment with ideologies and existing social structures, of a search for new ideals, of detachment and alienation from self and others, there has arisen a profound longing for a delineation, expression, and affirmation of the self. The proliferation of many forms of psychotherapy, especially of those oriented toward an experiential approach, attests to the existence of this need. So, also, does the emphasis on self-expression, on creativity, and on the wish of each individual to "do his thing." That these attempts often miscarry, or are exaggerated or chaotic in form, has no bearing on the fact that the need for the individual will to assert itself exists. One might hazard the guess that the dissolution of tradition—the partial disintegration of society as we have known it— leaves the individual with little anchorage for identification with the social milieu. He is, therefore, thrown back upon himself and the necessity for building his own personality out of new, self-created ideals which will ultimately, through interaction with society, reconstitute a new community.

It is inevitable that in the uncertainty of such a transitional period, individual conflicts will arise for which the understanding of Rank's approach is particularly suitable.

Aside from Rank's timeliness in terms of the current social and psychological needs, his contributions to developmental psychology belong to the present rising tide of interest and research in the earliest manifestations of individuality, in the conflicts and problems caused by the inevitability of the child's separation from the mother. The original

Freudian theory of personality development was primarily a theory of psychosexual development embued with a patriarchal phallocentric point of view. Briefly, its model and point of departure was the small boy's sexual rivalry with his father for his mother, the ensuing castration anxiety which was thus aroused, and the resolution of this conflict through the boy's identification with his father's prohibition, which resulted in the development of the superego. The theory of the little girl's development is derived from that of the boy by way of tortuous and not very convincing processes of reasoning. The importance of the mother–child relationship for the development of personality comes late in the history of psychoanalysis.

Rank was ahead of his time both in perceiving the centrality of this relationship and in emphasizing the importance of separation from it as a source of conflict in the process of individuation. Subsequently in the work of Melanie Klein and her followers, and more recently in the works of Escalona, Bowlby, Mahler, Kohut and others, we find validation for Rank's conclusions—conclusions which Rank based on observations of his patients and on the intuitive depth of his self perceptions.

THREE

Creativity as the Central Concept in Rank's Psychology

I N THE early aloneness of his introspection, of his self-education, and of his struggle to transcend his childhood milieu, Rank became aware of the creative thrust of his own personality. This awareness led him to focus on creativity in its broadest meaning as the central concept in his understanding of humanity. For him the creative process manifested itself in the formation and unfolding of personality itself, as well as in the productive work of the artist. Yet the artist's creativity, as the most dramatic example of man's striving for self expression, growth, and change, led Rank to select the artist as the exemplar of the creative experience. He did not wish to "explain" the artist or his work in causal psychological terms; instead, he wished to apply his perception of the operation of the creative process, as he observed it in the artist, to the understanding of human psychology in general—in fact, to life as a whole. He says explicitly: "Creativeness lies equally at the root of artistic production and of life experience."[1]

Even in his first work, *Der Künstler,* in which he was strongly under the influence of his reading of Freud, Rank thinks in interactional terms. He is concerned with the movement and progression to higher levels of conscious awareness of the individual and of the culture in which he lives, as the creative forces existing in both are expressed and mutually influence each other. He refers to the sublimated work of the individual as not only expressing his own creative need, but also that of society (pp. 50–53).

Rank, philosophical process thinker that he is, sees a progressive, creative process underlying all the phenomena of life. Both in individual and collective terms, life processes are in evolution, spurred on by a creative impulse. This in turn is released by an inevitable duality in life itself: the duality represented by a movement toward individuation on the one hand and a need to remain part of a larger whole on the other. In human life this results in a psychological conflict which the individual can resolve through the functioning of his creative will—a term which Rank coined and with which we shall deal in detail in the next chapter.

Rank's view of life is confirmed in a profoundly brilliant and poetically expressive work of Susanne Langer[2] in which she draws upon biological data and documents the operation of the creative evolutionary process throughout all of animate nature, as it manifests itself in two processes: individuation and involvement.

> To trace the development of mind from the earliest forms of life that we can determine, through primitive acts which may have vague psychical moments, to more certain mental acts, and finally the human level of "mind," requires a more fertile concept than "individual," "self," or even "organism;" not a categorial concept, but a *functional* one, whereby entities of various categories may be defined and related. The most promising operational principle for this purpose is the principle of *individuation*. It is exemplified everywhere in animate nature, in processes that eventuate in the existence of self-identical organisms. . . .
>
> Under widely various conditions, this ubiquitous process may give rise to equally various kinds of individuality, from the physical self-identity of a metabolizing cell to the intangible but impressive individuality of an exceptional human being.

Langer shares with Rank a profound appreciation of the creative life force which brings about the individuation of autonomous entities on all levels of the evolutionary process, while at the same time producing an unlimited measure of variety among individuals.

It is the very uniqueness of the individual that leads Rank to the seemingly paradoxical statement that a purely individual psychology cannot explain personality, for by individual psychology he means a generalized psychology derived from a study of individuals. Some general psychological facts about personality may be contributed by such a psychology, but the particularity of an individual cannot be reduced causally to generalized psychological dynamics.

Rank uses as a striking example the attempt to explain genius psychologically, which he feels must inevitably misfire: first because one cannot "explain" personality, and second because the genius is the maximum expression of the productive personality at its most characteristically individual, and is therefore subject to the greatest variability and unpredictability.[3] He writes: the "psychology of personality has helped little or not at all" in understanding the genius. "Moreover, it probably never will contribute anything, since ultimately we are dealing with dynamic factors that remain incomprehensible in their *specific* expression in the *individual personality*. This implies that they can be neither predetermined nor wholly explained even ex post facto."[4]

What a blow to a deterministic theory of personality! What respect for the uniqueness of the individual; for the emphasis in Rank's perception of creativity as it expresses itself either in the work of the productive personality, or in the creation of personality itself, is on the specificity of this expression in the individual personality, in other words, on what has become individuated. Certainly we can arrive at some psychological generalizations, as Rank himself does. But his awareness of the almost infinite variability and diversity of individual persons is an indication of his sensitivity to the creative aspect of the evolutionary life process. As C. J. Herrick has noted: "This diversity is manifested first in the biological process of evolution through the chance rearrangement of chromosomes when, in fertilization in a specific instance, the paternal and maternal chromosomes are paired," so that "no two people in the world (except identical twins) are exactly alike genetically, and these innate differences are accentuated by the diverse cultural influences to which they respond."[5]

The uniqueness of individuals results in an individual expression of creative will which can be neither predetermined nor predicted in its specific detail. It can only be accepted as a manifestation of the life process.

But just as life itself in the biological sense struggles to emerge, persist, and reproduce in the face of the disintegrating forces of entropy in the universe, so in the creation of personality and in the creation of the products of personality (artistic, literary, philosophic, scientific) various forms of duality are responsible for analogous struggles.

There is in man precisely because he is a self-conscious, sensate creature, and is therefore able to create his unique personality, an urge to eternalize it. Thus the duality between his individual mortality and his wish for immortality becomes an inevitable aspect of human life.[6] The wish for immortality is expressed in the artistic creation of the individual as well as in the creation of religious forms and other social institutions. The latter is a communal immortality, the former an individual one. Thus, out of the individual's mortality–immortality conflict, a new duality arises, especially for the creative artist—that between individuality and collectivity.

It is in his book *Art and Artist,* especially in the chapter entitled "Creative Urge and Personality Development," that Rank spells out in detail the nature and consequences of the mortality–immortality conflict in relation to other dualities to which it gives rise. Rank uses the artist as an *example* of the operation of creativity while realizing that his insights apply to all forms of creative expression, not least to the creation of the self.

The individual artist is born into a specific culture within a given epoch. This sociohistorical situation, an outgrowth of the cumulative effects of sociocultural evolution, provides him with its characteristic art form or style, with a given cultural ideology, with its store of scientific knowledge. To express something personal—i.e., to satisfy his need for immortality—he uses the given cultural form; but in so doing he also adds or alters something so that his product differs sufficiently from the cultural cliché as to be his own individual creation. Ultimately the expression of his individuality and that of many creative individuals acts upon the whole cultural ideology so as to alter it. This interplay between creative personality and cultural form, ideology, and institutions advances sociocultural evolution. For the individual creative personality, however, it represents the conflict between the dualism of individuality and collectivity.

The dualism, individuation–involvement, which Langer describes as characterizing the life process, and in which individuation refers to the emergence of "self-identical organisms" and involvement to the interaction, communication, or integration of organisms with one another, is akin to Rank's dualism of "individuality and collectivity." For Rank realized the impact of social processes upon the individual who, in the process of structuring his personality, seeks, on the one hand, to emerge from the nexus of collective forces, and, on the other, wishes to lose himself within the whole. For just as the growing child must create his personality out of a synthesis of individual experience with the socio-historical reality into which he is born, so the artist must wrest his unique-ness from the collectivity in which he finds himself and yet create a product which is in harmony with his culture.

Rank was profoundly sensitive to the conflict aroused by this duality. At a much later date, with no awareness of Rank's earlier contribution to an understanding of the creation of personality via the exploration of the artist's struggle to synthesize his individual expression within the context of his historical setting, Erik Erikson, writing about the for-mation of ego-identity, says: "The growing child must derive a vitalizing sense of reality from the awareness that his individual way of mastering experience (his ego synthesis) is a successful variant of a group identity and is *in accord* with its space-time and life plan."[7] However, as I have remarked in another connection, "For psychological and sociocultural evolution to take place, for there to be any 'gains' which can then be consolidated into socially usable and transmissible form, the individual ego, or at least the egos of a sufficient number of individuals within a culture, must advance *beyond* what could be regarded as a 'successful variant' within the group to a higher degree of individuation, thus form-ing foci from which the diffusion of higher levels of organization into the group as a whole can take place."[8] Through his emphasis on crea-tivity, Rank had already pointed out that increasing individualization as it interacts with collectivity alters the whole cultural ideology and there-fore art with it.

There is another aspect of the dualism of individual and community which brings into sharp relief the nature of the creative impulse; that is the dualism in psychological form between self-assertion and self-renunciation. According to Rank the creative urge is self-assertive; the experience of aesthetic pleasure is its opposite, self-renunciation; the individual loses himself in the enjoyment of a communally affirmed creation. While such renunciation of self may be an *aspect* of the psy-chology of the aesthetic experience, it would scarcely serve as a total description of that experience in the eyes of philosophers of aesthetics. For example, Flaccus sees within the aesthetic experience a sort of secondary creating in response to the artist's creative work: "The artist gives himself in his work; he offers a personal interpretation—we who respond to what the artist gives, read it whether we will or no in psychic terms. A few patches of color and strokes, a few sequences of sounds, a few words is all that we need to set us off on this enriching. We must see to it, however, that we are always in harmony with what of psychic value the artist has built into his picture, his poem, his symphony." (Perhaps this aspect of the act of aesthetic experiencing corresponds to what Rank refers to as self-renunciation.) "The double process, then, of creating and moving within a world of semblance, and of enriching the images and shapes of that world with our psychic wealth yields the meaning of the aesthetic experience."[9] In art the dualism of individual and community is reflected in both the uniqueness of expression of the artist and the collectively dictated style of an epoch.

In relation to creativity Rank points out another duality, a seemingly paradoxical one—that between life and creation. He does not mean that life lacks creativity; quite the contrary. But in discussing this duality, for the artist especially, he attempts to differentiate the artist's life of actuality, his transient experience, that which is ephemeral, from the sought-after eternalization in his creative product. The artist tries to protect himself from the transiency of experience by creating in some form a concretization of his personality, thereby immortalizing his mortal life. For the average man such immortalization is achieved through participation in or identification with the creative cultural ideology of his time, be it religious, political, scientific, or artistic.

The conflictful relationship between the immediate and the eternal, between the ephemeral and the enduring, between experience and artistic creation, can never be totally resolved. In fact, it is in the nature of the life process itself, in growth, in change, and in creation, to battle continuously with this duality. It is the creative urge, expressed through the individual will, that at one and the same time produces the conflict and attempts its resolution through all the manifestations of creativity.

The dualities which Rank sees as crucial in the life of man—that between mortality and immortality, between individuality and collectivity, between transient experience and artistic creation—lead to a psychology of personality quite different from that of Freud. It is a psychology essentially existential in character, in which the inevitable conditions of life itself impinge upon the formation of personality and in which the creative urge expresses itself volitionally both in the structuring of personality and in its creative products. It is a psychology of the self, and the dualities and the conflicts which they precipitate are those from which the self must emerge. The self is propelled into such emergence essentially by the life-impulse which is creative.

Freud perceived the duality of impulse and inhibition; of conscious and unconscious, and later of ego and id. That which propelled the individual toward maturation and toward the formation of ego was basically the need for the reduction of energic tension—in Freud's terms, the pleasure principle and its modification, the reality principle. True, the instinctual drives which dominated the life of the individual could be tamed, their gratification postponed, their aims diverted. Sublimation of libidinal drives was held to be the source of creativity and therefore of its products. For Freud the drives were primary; for Rank creativity was primary, deriving from the life-impulse and serving the individual will.

The volitional aspect of creativity is crucial for the production of an art work which is to express the unique individuality of the artist. However, before the artist can fashion the product of his creative impulse he must create himself, for the first work of the productive individual is the creation of his own artistic personality. Here Rank describes a most interesting phenomenon—the appointment of the artist by himself as artist. This is a spontaneous manifestation of the creative impulse. It is as if the first creative endeavor of the artist were a self-definition, a statement of his self-conception. It is a self-conception which is a glorification of his personality, unlike the neurotic who is either overly self-critical or overidealizing, and who is overly dependent for his self-image on others. The ability to appoint oneself is an act which reflects one's individuation, one's emergence from the matrix of childhood dependency. It is the precondition in the average individual for the creation of a mature, separate personality, and for the creative artistic personality it is the first productive work. The subsequent works of the artist are in part repeated expressions of this primal creation and in part justifications of it through the dynamism of work. For while an artist's work rests on the precondition of the glorification of his individual personality, he is called upon within his own psychic life to justify his individual creation through work and ever higher achievement.

This is because creation, whether in the form of an art work or in the fashioning of an autonomous self, is an act of individuation, of separation. As such it is achieved at the expense of "the other"—be that mother, the family, or society at large.[10] The resultant guilt must be expiated and the creative artist can do this through social justification of his work. Rank understood profoundly the relationship between individuation and the wish to merge and emphasized the fact that guilt is the inevitable accompaniment of all manifestations of creativity and therefore an inevitable fact of existence.

The problem of justification for the creative individual brings his self-appointment into juxtaposition with the values and ideology of the society in which he lives and creates. For his self-appointment can only succeed in a society which recognizes and values his individual creation; or, as Rank would phrase it, a society which has an ideology of genius, an appreciation of individualism in contrast to collectivism, or at least of some individualism within a predominantly collectivist framework. Today we have a striking example of this interaction between the artist and his social justification in the case of Solzhenitsyn, whose self-appointment was not valued, was in fact denounced and persecuted, in the Soviet Union. The tremendous strength of his individuality made it possible for him to create even in the face of active social opposition, but he had ultimately to seek a milieu which was congenial to his conception of himself as a creative artist—a milieu in which he could justify himself and his work.

Rank is critical of psychological attempts to "explain" the artist's work by an interpretation of his past experience. It is not experience but the reaction to experience which is crucial. Only the creative impulse, i.e. the will to create interacting with the social milieu, can explain the inner dynamism through which the creative work is born. However, since personality itself is the product of a creative endeavor, we would assume that Rank, when interpreting the nature of individual personalities, would place the emphasis not so much upon the history of past experiences as upon the strength of creative will which is accessible to each individual in the task of assimilating experience.

The impulse to create originates in an inherent striving, in Rank's terms, toward totality—toward what we would call ever higher and more complex levels of integration. This tendency is no less characteristic of the psychic life of man than of living matter in general. It is a process which takes place in the conflictful context of a duality between a surrender to life and an urge toward a creative reorganization of experience.

Rank makes an interesting distinction between the artist and the neurotic individual in relation to the fate of the creative impulse. The artist succeeds, to a greater or lesser degree, in overcoming the traumas of childhood, in reducing guilt and anxiety, and in minimizing the existential conflict between the awareness of his own mortality and the wish for immortality. He achieves this in two ways: through the creation of a concrete product expressive of his individuality, and through his creative attitude toward himself and the inevitabilities inherent in the nature of life itself. Through an act of will he is able to say "yes" to these inevitabilities. Rank calls this "the volitional affirmation of the obligatory." It is precisely this last mentioned creative act which certain neurotics are unable to perform. Rank calls such individuals *artistes man-qué's.*[11] They are inhibited in the exercise of the positive will to create. His therapy, therefore—which he came to call will therapy—focuses primarily, not on a causal understanding of early experience and the implementation of insight gained thereby, but instead addresses itself to a re-experiencing of the anxiety and guilt which has stunted the creative will of the individual and through affirmation of this will in the therapeutic interaction seeks to free it to function positively and creatively. It is thus creativity which stands in the center of Rank's theory and therapy, and which ultimately serves man in the resolution of conflict.

FOUR

The Will

Agent of the Creative Force

L IKE the nautilus which, having outgrown its old abode, builds new chambers to accommodate its growth, so Otto Rank structured his understanding of human problems through creatively overcoming the confines of his own emotional struggles. He was deeply depressed in the early years of his adulthood and the fear of death haunted him. He wrote: "Death, the mysterious phenomenon that many thinking people have attempted to explain, became a problem to me above all. I still remember that I did not sleep for many nights and thought only about dying with terror and chattering teeth."[1] His isolation, withdrawal, even aversion for people reached such proportions that in this despair he wrote a long letter that might be called an appeal for help to an unmentioned individual. (Taft thinks the letter was never sent but that Rank may have had a particular person in mind.)[2] The writing of this letter, which was an admission to himself of his need for human contact, marked a turning point in the resolution of his conflict.

Such struggles during adolescence or early adulthood are not uncommon; yet in the case of Rank it is the nature of their resolution which is of extreme importance for an understanding of the contributions to psychology which he was to make later. In spite of his despair, he had an "unbreakable faith" in his talents. He turned his fear of death and his struggle with life into a creative act, first through the creation of his own personality and ultimately the creation of his psychology of creativity and of the will; and he based a psychotherapy as well as a philosophy of life on these theories. It was the reality of this personal experience that convinced him of the productive value of experience as against mere understanding. He acquired a sense of the indomitable life force, fighting against death to immortalize, to perpetuate itself, through the exercise of the will, in some expression, tangible or psychological, of the creative impulse.

It is little wonder that Rank's psychological preoccupations began with a concern with the artist and with creativity. He was himself an artist in the broadest sense of that term, a master of poetic writing, a man of great aesthetic sensitivity, and philosophical imaginativeness, and a man committed to introspection. He sought to observe his own growth and to further it by absorbing the intellectual and emotional nutrition which contact with the writings of great thinkers afforded him. He was a man hungry for an ego-ideal, searching constantly for what he could assimilate and make his own in the creative process of building himself. In view of the emotional poverty of his background, we might well wonder about the source of his ultimate faith in his capabilities which formed the foundation upon which his self-architecture was based. And in the answer to this wonder, we must conclude that Rank's own answer in terms of the human will has great validity. One's image of oneself, one's faith in oneself, and one's capacity to act upon this faith is not only the product of identification with the image of oneself as it is projected by a loving parent, but also the result of an original, uniquely human "given" in the form of the will, which is representative of the life force.

It is common knowledge among psychologists familiar with psychoanalytic history and among those who have concerned themselves with Freudian theory and with Freud's personality that his mother had an overriding faith, amounting almost to superstition, in the inevitable greatness that was to be the destiny of her son. "My Golden Siggie," she enthused. Undoubtedly Freud incorporated this image of himself into his own personality and it gave him a sense of security and sustained him through difficult and discouraging periods. In working with patients, we find that it is often the absence of this positive image of self as it derives from parents to which we attribute lack of security, of independent judgment and productivity, and a slavish subservience to others.[3]

The life and work of Rank opens up another dimension of human potentiality. The unique and individual will of every person exists at the outset irrespective of childhood history and can be drawn upon to form the personality. And so while it is true that the human ego is in large measure shaped by the precipitates of early identifications, it is also true that it can be formed by the will which creatively helps the ego to build itself. By way of illustration, one might say that Freud *fulfilled* his mother's prophetic image of him through his creative achievements; Rank, on the other hand, *created* the very prophecy upon which he built his personality, and out of which then grew his productive achievements. In 1905, close to the time during which he was working on *Der Künstler*, he experienced his own will through the awareness of his capacity for growth and change. "The will expresses itself through the act of becoming born," he wrote; by which he meant psychological birth—the implementation in action of the ever renewed consciousness of differentiation between the self and its surround.

Let us try to formulate the essential features of Rank's theory of the will. His very choice of the term "will" and his preoccupation with the function of "willing" show him to be at variance with the prevailing thinking of his time—in fact, in the field of psychology, with much of the thinking of our own time. The scientific discoveries of the late nineteenth and early twentieth centuries, as they represented a material culmination of rationalistic philosophies, permeated the spirit of that time with the scientific ethos: causal, mechanistic, deterministic, reductionistic. The prevailing hope in the psychological study of man was that his behavior, his thought processes, even his emotions could be reduced to primary, determined, and material causes in much the same way that one might reduce causal relationships in the physical world. Thus the underlying premise in a basic formal sense is the same for a behavioristic as for a psychoanalytic view of man,—that human personality is reducible to determinable causes however differently the two opposing schools of thought conceive of the *content* of such causes.

Rank's difference with this point of view goes far beyond the issue of content. While he does not deny the biological foundation upon which human psychology is based (he refers to it as the creature in man), his fundamental emphasis is on the uniquely human quality of consciousness and its consequences. With the emergence of consciousness, especially self-consciousness (self-awareness) and its expression in the exercise of the will, man himself becomes the beginning of a new series of causes. While natural science causality *does* operate in the realm of the psychic, it does so only to a limited degree. It is historical in character and can only interpret that aspect of the present which derives from the past, whereas according to Rank the actual psychic belongs to the present and is created by an individual act of will. "The causality principle means a denial of the will principle since it makes the thinking, feeling, and acting of the individual dependent on forces outside of himself and thus frees him from responsibility and guilt."[4]

Thus we conclude that for Rank there resides a causality *within* the individual so that every act is not reducible to the deterministic influence of past experience as cause, but is the product, in addition, of causes residing in the inherent nature and specifically individual character of his will. "Only in the individual act of will do we have the unique phenomenon of spontaneity, the establishing of a new primary cause."[5] The emphasis here should be on the word "individual," for it is in the fact of differences in individuality that the possibility of a freely arrived at act of will, unbound by any predictable stereotype of causality, resides. This flexibility of psychic functioning as it is expressed in the individual will is the essentially human quality that identifies man as the creator of himself and defines his relationship to outer reality.

It is interesting to note that while willing is human, it is the culmination of a biological tendency toward individuation which lends a plasticity to the adaptability of living organisms that is essential for survival. There is in all the individual events of the living world a uniqueness which distinguishes each one from the broad outlines of the general, species specific pattern of behavior. So, for example, "The completed nest, the spider's web, the act of mating, is attained by a train of acts *different in detail* on every occasion."[6] Thus, even in the natural science world, we reach a point at which events are no longer reducible to causal interpretation. However, the evolutionary process which brought about individual variation to deal with the detail of adaptation to a specific environmental situation in the plant and animal is an aspect of a total life process which responds selectively to the natural environment in terms of survival. It is unknown and unknowable to the individual creature, for there is no awareness, no consciousness. It is purely adaptive as distinguished from the human ability to voluntarily make choices and so to act upon them as to change outer reality as well as the self. It is this capacity which is vested in the will and which Rank refers to as creative in distinction to adaptive.

By way of contrast Freud was focused on the inhibition of will—although he never called the active agent of the personality "will," but rather ego. His discovery that individuals were not free to carry out their wishes, that, in fact, their wishes were often unclear and full of conflict for those driven by forces unknown to them, was a momentous contribution to the understanding of human psychology. Before Freud, mental illness had been looked upon as a weakness of the personality which could be overcome if the individual "wanted to"—if he exercised his "will" and his "will power." That the will could be crippled through the interaction of childhood experience with the individual's particular inherent makeup, and that this process could take place without the awareness of the individual, was unknown before Freud. This is the significance of the discovery of the unconscious.

But Freud's discovery did more than explain certain types and certain aspects of mental illness, for he considered that to a large extent the operation of dynamic unconscious factors took place in the behavior, thinking, and feeling of all human beings. To this extent he was deterministic in his view of man. In fact, rather than saying "we live," he claimed "The Id lives us." It is not hard to realize that while the discovery of unconscious motivation and its effect on conscious functioning was of the utmost importance and had definite validity (as has been empirically demonstrated through observations in and outside the therapeutic situation), it altogether obscured the fact that human beings can also be motivated by self-determined conscious impulses of the will. These represent the positive, striving growth principle inherent in life itself—in a word, the creative impulse. Just as Freud discovered much of the meaning and significance of unconscious factors through the analysis of his own dreams, so Rank perceived the power of the self-creating will in terms of his own experience—the experience of transcending his milieu, that is, of not duplicating the lives of his forebears, but of creating his own according to his own lights; and subsequently, throughout various phases of his growth and development, of transcending himself. His own experience of the creative will in himself made him place such experience at the center of his therapeutic procedure—although he never denied the existence or unconscious factors.

According to Rank, the individual will has a negative character in terms of its origins. It begins as counter-will, as a "not wanting to," finding its strength in opposition. Although Rank does not trace this process through the developmental phases of childhood, observations of children certainly confirm the initial appearance of will, i.e., the assertion of individuality, as an oppositional phenomenon. This is the well-known contrary period between the ages of two and four.[7] The emphasis is on the child's need to assert his own individuality, to exercise his own will, even if it must be in opposition to his mother's.[8] In Rank's view the striving for individuation is primary; it is a given, expressed in the individual ego's creative seeking after higher goals. To quote Rank, the ego is the "temporal representative of the cosmic primal force; . . . the strength of this force represented in the individual we call the will."[9]

In referring to the "cosmic primal force," we understand Rank to mean, not some mystical power, but the energic nature of the universe, especially of the living universe. This force manifests itself in the human (because of consciousness and self-consciousness) not solely in adaptation to environment, but in a psychological interchange between inner and outer reality which can result in a freely chosen modification of either or both. It is such action which Rank calls creative as distinguished from adaptive, and which he comprehends as will phenomena.

In this definition Rank is attempting to distinguish what is characteristically human from what is animal. In the animal world behavior is largely patterned, having evolved (through countless ages) automatic, instinctual responses to the environment in order to guarantee the survival of the species. There is little here that is individually "chosen," although the potentiality for it exists in the uniqueness of each organism and of each environmental situation. This potentiality comes closer to realization the higher we ascend in the animal scale, so that when we reach the primates we can begin to see evidences of individually willed actions. Although there are certainly aspects of the animal creature in the psychology of the human being, Rank chose as the basis for his psychology that which is peculiarly human, namely the capacity for creative action.

The ability to act creatively, that is to choose to structure or alter the external environment as well as the self, is implemented through another human capacity: internalization. The outer world, of experience by way of memory, can become a part of the ego. This takes place in the course of development through identification with parental figures or others who influence the child during his growth. But Rank emphasizes that such identifications are added to what is originally the individual's own ego and that together they form an independent power. The force of this power is projected onto the outer world and is expressed as will, which manifests itself in the effort to influence and alter both the external world and the ego itself. In doing this it brings about as close a correspondence between inner and outer reality as possible.[10]

The expression of will, which has had its origins as negative will—as counter will—inevitably takes place in relation to another individual, to a social or cultural situation, to life circumstances, or to some contravening aspects of the personality itself. In other words, although it exists as a primary force within the individual, in its functioning as the ultimate expression of individuality it must emerge under the pressure offered by the challenge of an obstacle. It is the vehicle for individual differentiation, for separation of self from "the other" or from the mass. This process of separation through the exercise of the will gives rise to guilt and to fear, which are inescapable aspects of life itself.

Rank refers to guilt as an *ethical* problem characteristic of every human relationship. It is important to note that Rank differentiates "ethical" from "moral." They are not opposites but represent a developmental continuum in our capacity for ideal formation—an innate capacity essential for our functioning as social beings. The development of this capacity hinges on our relationship to the expression of our own will, to the affirmation of this will which, because it is inevitably in *opposition* to the will of "the other," initially the mother, produces guilt feeling. Morality is man-made, through the internalization of specific social and cultural customs, mores, and laws to form the superego.

The ethical conflict in human life is *originally* a biological given in terms of the child's tie to the mother from which he must separate in order to become an individual in his own right. This separation is attended with guilt because it occurs at the expense of "the other." Since every subsequent human relationship as well as each succeeding phase of development in the course of the maturation of personality represents a struggle between the wish to be separate and the wish to merge, the ethical conflict is repeated throughout life:

> Separation is one of the fundamental life principles. All organic evolution itself rests upon separation, but only the conscious knowledge of this life principle on the part of man who can preserve or call back the past in his memory, or can imagine the future in his phantasy, gives to the concept and the feeling of separation the fundamental psychic meaning. This explains why the first biological separation of the individual from the mother *can acquire* the psychic meaning that I ascribe to it in the "Trauma of Birth," likewise why all further steps on the way to self-dependence, such as weaning, walking, and especially the development of the will, are conceived always as continuous separations, in which the individual even as in the last separation, death, must leave behind, must resign developmental phases of his own ego.[11]

It is not so difficult to understand that separation is a source of anxiety. The human infant is born in a completely helpless state and is totally dependent on the mother for survival. Her absence, initially experienced by the dim perception of unmet survival needs—nourishment, warmth, contact—produces the terror of nonsurvival. As the child's consciousness of the world takes form, he becomes aware of the extent of his dependency. However, his slowly increasing developmental independence, his gradual mastery of the world, does not keep pace with the awareness of the extent to which he depends on others, especially on his mother. There is consequently a residual fear which is repeated throughout life in all significant relationships that are characterized by emotional dependency, and in all situations of separation which can become symbolic of this original dependency. In each individual case, the extent of such fear of separation will be governed by constitutional factors, by the specific nature and history of the relationship to the mother, and by the innate resources available to the individual for overcoming the fear.

However, Rank rarely uses the concept of dependency, nor does he trace in detail the maturational fate of the separation problem. His point of departure is always the will. Since will is the product of consciousness, especially consciousness of self, he is mainly concerned with understanding the relationship to the self of those forces in life with create conflict or inhibition in the functioning of will.

Human life, according to Rank, exists within the framework of a paradox—a fear of living and a fear of dying. The former constitutes a fear of becoming psychologically what the human being already is biologically, a unique and separate individual. The fear is that of isolation, of being on one's own, separate and responsible for one's own life. In the almost completely deterministically controlled animal world, survival fear has evolved phylogenetically as a signal of danger, together with the appropriate defensive behavior to deal with the danger. Each individual creature can rely on genetically patterned behavior, specific for its species. It does not have to appraise a situation, make judgments, and take appropriate action. In fact, because of the existence of awareness, but not of consciousness in the human sense of that word, it is *unable* to do so. Not so for humans.[12] We must become aware of the implications of a situation, deal with our own understanding of and emotional reactions to it, decide upon action, and experience reaction. This is the function of willing as it is evoked by the stimulus of an external situation. Often it is brought into play by inner stimuli. In either case, the exercise of will is an individual act—is, in fact, the act which in all its aspects defines individuality and thus creates a separate person. And it is the full responsibility of this separateness which often weighs heavily on the human personality. It is most likely experienced first as a burden, because of the anxiety which it evokes; and only through a learning process does it come to be experienced as an opportunity—an opportunity for the creative expression of the unique self. This is our understanding of what Rank means by life fear, and this, too, is experienced in its duality, for the fear of the birth of one's own individuality, as it is expressed in willing, is balanced by an overpowering wish to live and to fulfill this wish through becoming the separate and unique individual which one has the potential to be—through the creative expression of one's will.

The individuated personality, so dearly bought at the price of overcoming the fear of separateness and the inevitable guilt associated with willing, the realization of its unique potentiality, is assailed by the conscious awareness of its transitory nature, of its mortality. The fear of death and its corollary, the wish for immortality, are indubitable psychological facts and, according to Rank, are strong motivating factors in the process of the creative implementation of the will.

Ernest Becker reveals a profound understanding of Rank's contribution to our insight into the nature of man's basic fears and to the defenses against them. Comparing these views with Freud's he writes:

> Man's body *was* "a curse of fate" and culture was built upon repression— not because man was a seeker only of sexuality, of pleasure, of life and expansiveness, as Freud thought, but because man was also primarily an avoider of death. *Consciousness of death* is the primary repression, not sexuality. As Rank unfolded in book after book and as Brown[13] has recently again argued, the new perspective on psychoanalysis is that its crucial concept is the repression of death. *This* is what is creaturely about man, *this* is the repression on which culture is built, a repression unique to the self-conscious animal.[14]

The dawn of consciousness marks the beginning of an awareness of its end. Often we encounter the awareness of death quite early in childhood, where it is inevitably met with great anxiety. Throughout history, the attempt to deal with this anxiety is revealed in myth and legends, in religion and, according to Rank, in the artistic products of creative individuals with whom the mass of people can identify. Paradoxically, the fear of death and its counterpart, the wish for immortality, lead to the fullest expression of life in the form of the creative expression of the will. That is not to say that the wish for immortality is the *cause* of creative action and its consequent product, but rather it motivates and mobilizes the striving for the expression of individuality which is a given and is there at the outset. This illustrates how Rank eschews a simple causal approach to the problems of human psychology and always thinks in terms of complex interactional and interrelated processes whose paradoxes we can only partially untangle.

Rank's contribution to the understanding of the psychology of the artist and of his creative impulse is monumental; but his understanding of the will of the average individual is profound in its implications for psychology and for therapy. For in the dual struggle for individuation and separation on the one hand, and against death and annihilation on the other, the will has the opportunity to create the self—to build the personality—and to affirm life as well as its inescapable companion, death. "To live fully, even to survive successfully, man must perform a *positive act of will* maximally. . . . First he must 'say yes' to life and this then becomes the creative aspect of adjustment; secondly, according to his capacity and the situation, he must effect change and bring forth the new; this is the adaptive aspect of creation."[15]

It is the inability to affirm his own will, as well as to affirm the obligatory aspects of life and to take responsibility upon himself for functioning within the limitations of this framework, that characterize the neurotic character. It therefore becomes the task of therapy to help the individual to free himself from the fear and guilt which have inhibited such affirmation, that is, to liberate his individual will.

This leads us to the issue of guilt in Rank's theory of personality. It is not easy to understand, because guilt which arises out of the wish to be oneself, to express oneself in creative ways, in other words, "to will," seems on the face of it irrational, and comprehension would call for some rational explanation. And, again, when we set aside our need for a rational explanation, the issue of guilt in connection with separation and creation is not easy to *feel* or to experience. The reason would seem to lie in the fact that it remains unconscious, or perhaps has been deeply repressed after having briefly reached consciousness. In either case, Rank does not deal with the unavailability to subjective consciousness of the experience of guilt in this connection. He does speak of consciousness of guilt, but he does not mean consciousness of wrongdoing in the Freudian sense of superego guilt. For the Freudian concept of conscience, and therefore of guilt for bad conscience, refers to a specific content; it is a self-criticism of wish, thought, or action measured against norms of morality which are socially determined. It is, therefore, a guilt which derives from without. For Rank, guilt is an inescapable aspect of the human condition and is therefore built into the personality as soon as the consciousness of individuality appears. As we said earlier, the process of individuation begins with the expression of will as counterwill: will expressed in opposition to that of parents on whom the child is dependent. In the name of self-assertion, the child must deny the gratitude which the meeting of his dependency needs by his parents calls forth, or must deny the denial of gratitude by expressions of love. Since such expressions arise secondarily and defensively, and are not the result of a differentiated and separate personality appreciating "the other," they inevitably give rise to guilt feelings. This is not guilt for the specific content of instinctual wishes, be they sexual or aggressive, as for example the wishes surrounding the Oedipus complex as understood by Freud—although such guilt exists. It is guilt for the very fact of being and of becoming as this is expressed in the act of willing to be separate. If the will is expressed in opposition to the other loved person, the guilt is ethical, in Rank's use of that term, to express the relationship of one individual to another. But will can also be expressed in a yielding, a surrender to the will of the other, not out of a will to give—which would be a healthy solution to the will conflict—but as a reaction to separateness, and then the guilt exists for the betrayal of one's own striving for individuation.

The problem of the inescapable will conflict and its accompanying guilt is at the very center of the therapeutic process, according to Rank, and we shall deal with his profound understanding of its intricacies and many dimensions, as well as with his conception of the therapeutic agent and its differentiation from the Freudian conception of what is therapeutically effective in chapter 10.

In the nonhuman animal world, the relationship between the species and the individual, and between individuals of the same species, has evolved to serve the survival, reproduction, and therefore perpetuation of the species. In the struggle of life for existence there is at this level no guilt, for there is no awareness of self or other, and therefore no possibility for empathic identification with another individual. With the birth of consciousness, both the self and the other are born psychologically and the capacity to project oneself into the situation of the other person, in fact the inevitability of so doing, brings self-interest into conflict with the will of the other. It is this will conflict which gives rise to guilt. This is what Rank means when he speaks of man as an ethical animal and sees guilt as his inescapable destiny.

Philosophers and religious thinkers have been aware of this human dilemma throughout the ages. As W. Macneile Dixon has noted:

So, early in human history, the will-to-live was challenged—How to justify, men began to ask, their own seizure of the best, or how the conflicting purposes, their own with all the others, were to be harmonized, strife evaded, hatreds avoided, wars ended, unbroken happiness attained—How, in the face of this universal conflict, is the individual to secure his own ends, how to exist, expand, realize his innermost, his profoundest needs, without

interference with lives and purposes no less justifiable than his own, without
injury to them, without the destruction or subjugation of the rest, the vast
concourse of other living creatures? Each and all, you and I, have their
moral rights to what existence offers. Every man has his case and his claims
as undeniable as those of his neighbors. They have not been answered, those
questions, not one of them.[16]

It was the awareness of the implications of consciousness as expressed
through the will function of the individual ego, as it came in conflict
with the will of others and thus led inevitably to guilt, that made Rank
place this conflict in a central position in his psychology and caused him
to see guilt as the inescapable accompaniment of the human condition.
The power of will is equal to the influences of the outer environment
and to the claims of the inner instinctual life. The will, Rank notes,

is not only able to suppress the sex-urge, but is just as able to arouse it
through conscious effort, to increase it and to satisfy it. Perhaps our will
is able to do this because it, itself, is a descendant, a representative, of the
biological will-to-live become conscious, creating itself in self-maintenance
and reproduction, which in the last analysis is nothing more than supra-
individual self-maintenance. When this tendency to perpetuate self-maintenance of the species carries over to the individual there results the powerful
will whose manifestations bring with them guilt reactions because they
strive for an enrichment of the individual, biologically at the cost of the
species, ethically at the expense of the fellow man.[17]

By bringing the issue of will out from unjustified philosophical obscurity into the psychological arena as will conflict, Rank has given us
a deepened insight into the ever-present problems of anxiety and guilt.
By emphasizing the striving, creative aspects of will, he has pointed a
way to the amelioration, if not the solution, of these human problems
and in the application of these insights concerning will to the therapeutic
process, he has introduced a new understanding of the effective therapeutic agent and a new technical approach for helping the individual
patient.

FIVE

On Guilt

RANK'S UNDERSTANDING of guilt in human experience is unique in psychoanalytic psychology and utterly profound. It derives, as we have already seen, from his understanding of will and from his deep appreciation of the implications of consciousness and of the struggle for autonomy in the development of the self. However, while the awareness of these issues informs Rank's thinking from the beginning, he struggled to clarify his thoughts throughout his life. As a result, in studying Rank's views on guilt we encounter a progression from his early point of view expressed in *Sexualität und Schuldgefühl* (Sexuality and Guilt Feeling) and Grundzüge einer *Genetischen Psychologie*, both not fully translated works published in the years 1926 and 1927, to the existential perspective expressed in his last work, *Beyond Psychology*, published posthumously in 1941. The progression represents a gradual shift from the libido theory of Freud as the point of departure to the understanding of guilt in ego psychological terms as the inevitable price for the emergence of individuality, and of its amelioration through creative work. Thus Rank ultimately relates guilt to the function of "willing" and to the fact that it is an unavoidable byproduct of the process of individuation.

This development in Rank's thinking throws light not only on the differences between Freudian and Rankian theory, and therefore on the evolution of psychoanalytic thought, but also illustrates Rank's emerg-

ence as an original thinker through the very process of individuation of
which he speaks.

The Genetic Psychology represents a bridge in Rank's theoretical development between the view of guilt as arising from sexual impulses and
guilt in its relationship to processes of ego formation. In this work Rank
was seeking the genetic roots of "ego states" such as guilt and anxiety,
and as we might expect from our knowledge of an earlier work, *The
Trauma of Birth* (which we will discuss in the next chapter), he turned
to an exploration of the early mother–child relationship for an explanation. It is important to remember that when we say "turned to the
early mother–child relationship" we are referring to his focus on observation in psychoanalytic work with adults and not to empirical studies.
For Rank, just as Freud, arrived at his insights derivatively from therapeutic work, from his creative, intuitive imagination. Rank also brought
to his work a vast knowledge of such cultural phenomena as myth,
legend, and art, which helped to build the theoretical framework around
which his observations of individuals were grouped.

According to Rank, at this point in his own development, guilt is *not*
primarily the legacy of the Oedipal triangle, as Freud taught; therefore
it is *not*, for the boy, the byproduct of the taboo surrounding the child's
sexual impulses toward his mother and the attempt to master these
through the internalization of his father's prohibition against the expression of these impulses. Such identification with the father's forbidding
stance is motivated by the fear of castration by the father as punishment
for these sexual urges. Guilt would thus result from an inner conflict
between unconscious incestuous sexual impulses and the internalized
prohibition against carrying them out. It becomes the deterrent for acting
upon them. This position places the origin of guilt feeling in the genital
phase of psychosexual development with castration fear as the motor for
the resolution of forbidden impulses.

In Rank's view guilt comes into being much earlier in human development—in fact within the earliest phases of interaction between mother
and child. To begin with, there are biologically given, primarily oral-
sadistic impulses which become dammed up because of self-inhibiting
processes. These inhibitions are motivated by the libidinal attachment
to and the consequent fear of separation from the mother who is experienced as all-powerful, both giving and depriving. Since Rank un-

derstands that the inevitable frustrations and deprivations the child must experience very early in his relationship to the mother are essential for ego formation and psychological growth, the self-inhibition of destructive, sadistic impulses must occur out of fear that were the child to act on them, he would lose the mother on whom he is dependent and to whom he is libidinally attached. The unavoidable deprivations of child-rearing by bringing about inhibition of impulse provide the groundwork for the child's perception and acknowledgement of his mother as separate and different. The cleavage between inner and outer world is thereby created.

Added to the fate of hostilities eventuating in guilt, which arise in the earliest oral phase of development, are those which emerge during the anal phase, when the strict prohibitions of the mother (who prescribes cleanliness) are met with resentment and rebellion on the part of the child. These feelings are initially expressed as stubborn contrariness which Rank was later to describe as "negative will." But sexual guilt also has its origin in the anal phase. The strict prohibitions are carried over in relation to genital impulses, but the hatred of the mother, with its attendant guilt, does not derive *primarily* from anger over the restraining of these impulses, but from the rage which ensues for her control and curbing of the narcissistic gratifications the child experiences as compensations for the loss of satisfactions both on the anal and genital levels.

Guilt arises not through identification with a forbidding father but as a precipitate of ego formation through separation from the mother. But the inhibition of the biologically given oral sadistic impulses results also in the need for some discharge of these hostile impulses toward the mother and they are turned against the self in the form of the need for punishment. The child incorporates the strict mother image as a part of his own ego which demands punishment out of guilt for his sadistic impulses. This internalization and the taking of the guilt upon oneself perpetuates the relationship to the mother and stands in the way of separation from her. It also forms the kernel of the superego for both men and women. Thus the superego in Rank's theory is not the product of a direct identification with a forbidding parental figure from fear of castration, which creates a *structure* within the personality as in Freud's theory, but the result of the incorporation of a *process* of relatedness to the mother—a strict mother who continues to arouse guilt within the individual as the price paradoxically for separating and for avoiding separation from her. Rank presages the later object relations theorists (Fairbairn, Winicott, Guntrip) in his awareness of the mother–child relationship, especially as it focuses on the issue of separation in ego formation.

In cases in which the mother is not strict enough the child seeks to ameliorate guilt for the inevitable hostilities toward her by a discharge of aggression which is calculated to provoke punishment—a mechanism frequently encountered in the behavior problems of children.

It is interesting that in speaking of "dammed up" sadistic impulses and the need for their discharge, which is an energic emphasis in the conception of personality, Rank's thinking in *The Genetic Psychology* remains within the framework of Freudian instinct theory. Yet even here in his emphasis on the issue of separation from the mother as indispensable for the structuring of the self, he is an ego psychologist. Within this process it is the *relationship* to the mother and the fear of loss of this relationship for which guilt is the building factor.

It is interesting that Rank, whom we might regard as the most philosophical of depth psychological thinkers, reverts at this phase of his own development to biological sources for an understanding of the genesis of guilt feelings. For fundamentally, while guilt arises in the emotional interaction of mother and child it does so because of the child's need, out of his dependency, to inhibit biologically given destructive impulses. Thus guilt leads back beyond all memory, beyond psychology to the biological, and all attempts to explain it are in essence rationalizations on various levels of libido development.[1]

Yet as Rank deepened his own understanding of the human dilemma he continued to explore the problem of guilt and to relate it to the will, to separation and to creativity. Gradually he departed more and more from libido theory as his conception of psychology left a linear, causal approach and became multidimensional, descriptive, and existential. His view is imbued with a sense of the inevitability of certain psychological life processes and with a profound acceptance of them. For Rank the psychological life is an intricate process in which many threads are interwoven to produce a tapestry in which the picture may vary from individual to individual and from culture to culture, but the pattern of the weave maintains an integrated relationship among the threads.

Thus guilt and will are threads which are inextricably enmeshed. To "will" is to assert oneself, to become individuated, to separate oneself from "the other"—originally the mother. In other words, to be born psychologically. As we have noted, the burden of the act of willing is fear and guilt, because the expression of will originates developmentally as counter-will within the context of the mother–child relationship. In attempting to clarify Rank's attaching of guilt to hostility in the expression of counter-will, it must be understood that the guilt cannot arise over the hostility or over the opposition alone. It is not simply guilt for childhood contrariness or a defiance of parental authority. Such guilt comes later in development and is secondary. The guilt is there chiefly because of the inevitable nature of human relatedness originating in the mother–child relationship.

The character of the earliest mother–child relationship is but an echo of the oneness of the child and the womb. Although the physical separation occurs through the act of birth, the psychological separation has yet to take place. For the mother, the child is still an extension of herself; for the child, too, there is as yet no differentiation between himself and the mother. In the language of psychoanalysis, the relationship is a narcissistic one. As the child grows and develops, differentiation takes place; first on a perceptual level, then through the burgeoning of self-assertion in the volitional act of "willing." But a certain legacy of the earliest narcissistic relationship remains in the form of empathy. Paradoxically, we can emphathize with another individual, because initially we were one with "the other." We see in "the other" both an identity with and a difference from ourselves. Thus an inevitable conflict between self-assertion and empathic feeling arises whenever the will of an individual is in opposition to the will, wishes, and needs of another. It is at the nodal point of this conflict that guilt feeling arises. Guild is a confession of the narcissistic origin both of self-assertion through separation and of empathy through union. But it can only come into being because of relatedness to another. It is the inescapable hallmark of human relatedness, and it is made possible by the emergence of consciousness. For it is when the condemnation of a specific *content* of the will is transferred to the *act* of will itself that the individual, through a disavowal of his own will because of empathic feeling for another, achieves a consciousness of guilt.

While Rank views guilt as deriving in the main from the will to separation, he movingly describes both the separating and uniting emotional aspects of guilt:

> I think the guilt feeling occupies a special position among the emotions, as a boundary phenomenon between the pronounced painful affects which separate and the more pleasurable feelings which unite. It is related to the painful separating affects of anxiety and hate. But in its relation to gratitude and devotion which may extend to self-sacrifice it belongs to the strongest uniting feelings we know. As the guilt-feeling occupies the boundary line between the painful and pleasureable, between the severing and uniting feelings, it is also the most important representative of the relation between the inner and the outer, the Ego and the Thou, the Self and the World.[2]

Rank's idea that guilt, if it is understood and accepted as existing unavoidably within the human condition, can be a uniting feeling because it derives from relatedness, is new in psychoanalytic theory. If an individual is able to accept guilt not only in himself, but as an expression of love, an expression of concern for him on the part of another, how much less unloved he might feel! For in learning to accept love in whatever form it is offered, the individual's ego becomes stronger and more differentiated. It is a strange, circular paradox of human psychology that guilt, a byproduct of the will to individuation, *when it is accepted rather than condemned*, should in itself become a vehicle for ego differentiation: in such acceptance within the self, the "other" is acknowledged as separate.

Clearly the binding force of guilt, even when it serves to unite, is not always positive. In clinical work, one frequently observes a period of depression (sometimes with strongly hypochondriacal features) at a time when we might least expect the emergence of symptoms of conflict or unhappiness: When the patient has realized many of his or her wishes— marriage, motherhood, professional success, the fulfillment of aspirations. As a therapist, one's first thought is of guilt over unconscious hostile feelings (generally toward a parent) and the accompanying punishment in the form of physical and psychic suffering. Since such feelings are an inevitable aspect of human development they are not hard to find. But an explanation in these terms is insufficient. It does not account for the intensity, the repetitive character and tenacity of the feelings, and even after the hostile feelings are uncovered and the supposed causality is interpreted and understood, the depressive, punitive, self-destructive mood of the patient persists. At this point, Rank's deeper understanding of guilt in relationship to separation becomes crucial.

A good example can be seen in the case of one of my patients. A young woman whose emotional history was replete with the legacy of an incompletely resolved symbiosis with her mother became acutely hypochondriacal some months after the birth of a little daughter. Her fear that her child would meet with some misfortune or die of some dire ailment frequently overwhelmed her. Herself a psychologist and a person of considerable insight, she attributed her anxiety to a re-evocation of her symbiotic ties to her mother, saying "I feel as if some part of me [the baby] was outside myself and as if I have no control over it." (See chapter 9 for another perspective.) The fear of separation from her mother as it is repeated in reverse with her own child is clear. The wish for the protection, security, and freedom from responsibility that such merging implies is also apparent. But wherein resides the guilt?

First it is important to realize that in both the wish and the fear there is a duality. The young woman wishes autonomy, but also wishes a loss of self; she fears the individuated role of the grown woman who has become a mother; but she also fears the loss of identity in a merging with her own internalized mother. The duality is not one of drive but is a split in the affective relationship of the self with the mother, so that if the ego acts upon one side of the split, it fails the other side.[3] In attempting to understand why guilt feelings should arise out of contradictory feelings it is important to remember that the mother has become internalized and that the contradictory duality originally existed within her. She herself was narcissistically overattached to her daughter (my patient) so that her own wish for maintaining the merged relationship, as well as her wish that her daughter should become an independent person, are reproduced in the self-structure of the young woman through processes of identification. The guilt of my patient arises because she cannot separate from her internalized, symbiotic mother and at the same time be true to the wish for a merging identity with her mother. In the sense that guilt arises within the context of a relationship, albeit internally within the unintegrated, split self, it is a social phenomenon and is therefore ethical in Rank's sense of that term.

The hypochondriacal symptom, which is the end product of this conflict in the case of my patient, is both punishment for the infidelity to the symbiosis and fear that the split and fragile self will totally disintegrate. The original lack of cohesiveness in the self is reinforced by the life circumstances that made my patient a mother before she resolved the separation–autonomy conflict with her own mother.

"How can I enjoy life when he or she is dead?" This frequently heard guilty outcry of individuals who have experienced the loss of a loved person appears from time to time in the therapeutic situation. The guilt is usually most readily explained in terms of the individual's unresolved ambivalence toward the loved one which manifested itself in some expressions of hostility, or in a lack of sufficient solicitousness. But this explanation of guilt, if it applies at all, accounts only for the most superficial level of the affect.

I am reminded of a patient who lost her mother during her psychoanalytic treatment. Their relationship had indeed been highly conflicted, but the guilt feelings which ensued upon the older woman's death did not abate until the issue of separation was addressed in her treatment. It became clear that the guilt was not primarily associated with self-reproach (for being, as the patient thought, insufficiently concerned or attentive to her mother's health in the last months of her life), but was fundamentally connected with her long and only partially resolved struggle to be separate and autonomous. The price for such autonomy would be the giving up of the narcissistic love of her mother—a need which was expressed in the transference in her wish that I regard her as a person of unuusual talent and intelligence. Symbolically, separation can mean not only hostility, but also the giving up of a certain kind of love—narcissistic love which presupposes idealization and oneness. It therefore implies separateness through the ability to get along on "realistic love" in terms of accepting the other person's capacities as well as the nature of one's own personality.

Guilt for the will to separate and to become autonomous and individuated poses a great threat to the helpless and dependent child. For some the fear of the separation from the mother and the guilt attendant thereon is so overwhelming that the child opts to give up "willing" almost entirely. The result is the maintenance of a symbiotic tie to the mother and a masochistic character structure in the child which persists throughout his or her life.[4]

Rank's perspective on guilt as an accompaniment of the individual will toward autonomy extends to an understanding of the role it has played in the history of culture. For while guilt arises in the individual person "toward others to whom he opposes himself through his individualization," universal guilt arises for man in his presumptuousness—in the hubris that results in the creative products of his culture. In religion, art, science and social structure mankind goes "beyond the limits set by nature."[5]

In the field of art, for example, when man is made uneasy by his own presumptuousness his creative efforts express themselves through an imitation of nature. This "betokens something like a rueful return to nature after too arrogantly rising above her, a self-imposed limitation on the individual presumption of creator."[6] It is this which makes Rank say "the ego is opposed to the world,"[7] and is therefore guilt-producing.

In a chapter in *Truth and Reality* entitled "Creation and Guilt,"[8] Rank portrays guilt as resulting from creation, and creation itself as the opportunity for redemption from guilt. The intertwined relationship of creation and guilt is brought about by man's consciousness when it goes beyond simple awareness and becomes an independent creative power challenging nature and human mortality. The evidence for such guilt is present throughout cultural history in the superstitions and rituals calculated to appease the existing gods and divert punishment in the form of natural disaster or death. Also in his religious and heroic myths man strives to account for his guilt in relationship to his conflict with God.

> The heroic myth strives to justify this creative will through glorifying its deeds, while religion reminds man that he himself is but a creature dependent on cosmic forces. So the creative will automatically brings the guilt reaction with it as the self-reducing depression follows the manic elation. In a word, will and guilt are the two complementary sides of one and the same phenomenon.[9]

In the life of an individual, guilt also arises for creation. A young writer revealed to me in the course of therapy that whenever he is profoundly involved in a piece of creative writing he becomes acutely hypochondriacal. The hypochondriacal fear attests to guilt and anticipates illness or death as punishment for the autonomous act of creation, an act which represents ultimate independence and therefore separation from parental introjects. Guilt arises in the wake of separation because the creative self assertion signals opposition to another part of the self which seeks oneness and merging with an internalized parental image. Thus guilt, as we have said before, arises in the face of the opposition inherent in a duality. Either the duality resides within the individual, or it exists in the opposition of the self to that of another. What then is the opposing duality in the case of creativity on a universal level—that creativity which has brought about humanity's great aesthetic and scientific achievements? According to Rank the duality is that between "human willing in contrast to natural being." This is "the root of the arch evil which we designate psychologically as guilt feeling."[10]

Humans are confronted by two basic issues, which come in conflict with autonomous creative will. One is the social, ethical issue: How to do justice to our own needs without injury to others? The other is a religious issue. How to temper creativity to keep it from becoming omnipotent, thereby destroying the much-needed God? For "God is not simply a deified father as Freud will have it, but an ideal created in man's image, in a word, a projection of the consciously willing ego."[11]

"This creative, omnipotent, omniscient God is the first great manifestation of the individual will, at the same time its denial and justification in the supra-individual world will, nature."[12] The common denominator in both conflicts is separation—fear of aloneness—especially of the ultimate separation, death. The creative expression of the will in its extreme form, since it represents self-interests, can thus lead to separation through the disavowal of our relatedness to our fellow human beings and through denial of our need for a power in the universe which transcends our own. Guilt arises because in serving our own needs for autonomy and immortality (served by creativity) we cannot also fully serve our ethical and religious needs—needs which our own consciousness has created.

If the expression of will in the creative act can bring about guilt feeling, it can also serve to expiate that guilt.[13] Through the acceptance of the inevitability of guilt and the knowledge that we cannot escape it, we can justify the guilt through our own creative action—i.e., through willing.

This seemingly circular reasoning becomes intelligible only if we realize, first, that in the acceptance and affirmation of our own will we are more true to ourselves than if we were to deny our will, and are therefore less guilty; and secondly, that the creative expression of will can take on a social form. We can create, as it were, for the love of the "other," and redeem the guilt for separation and opposition by returning to society what is needed, what is beautiful, what is lovable. Perhaps the universality and immortality of the greatest artists (for example, Bach), are a function of the degree to which their own unique individual creative will is merged with that of "the other" (in Bach's case, with the will of God). To see oneself as the vehicle for the expression of a will which transcends the self is to reduce the guilt for one's autonomous wishes.

Rank himself is exceptional in the fields of psychology and psychoanalysis in that his exploration of the guilt phenomenon is confined neither to sexual guilt nor to the dimension of the superego. Guilt for wishes— either sexual or aggressive—that are forbidden and come in conflict with the superego is only one, very limited aspect of the guilt experience. To have been able to see guilt in relation to processes of separation and individuation as these are expressed in the function of the will is Rank's unique contribution. But even more, he unearthed the strange paradox that when the will functions creatively it is guilt-producing, so that when the human creature becomes creator and masters or controls nature, on which he is ultimately dependent, he is inescapably guilty for his arrogant transcending. Since creativity is at the heart of Rank's view of man in the world, guilt must be its inevitable companion.

SIX

The Trauma of Birth
Reexamined

THE TRAUMA OF BIRTH is the work by which Rank is most often identified. This is unfortunate, since it represents but a phase in the development of his theory building and not the culmination of his thinking about the human situation. In writing this work he was moved to advance a theory of anxiety that would explain neurosis, create a bridge between the physical and the psychological, and thereby simplify and shorten the therapeutic process. Rank, at the time of the writing of *The Trauma of Birth* definitely thought of himself as a psychoanalyst, as an active member of the psychoanalytic community, and as a contributor to the growth of its body of knowledge. He wrote: "And so we would like to regard our arguments concerning the importance of the trauma of birth for Psychoanalysis only as a contribution to the Freudian structure of normal psychology, at best as one of its pillars. At the same time, we feel confident of having considerably furthered the doctrine of neuroses—including their therapy."[1]

Initially, Rank thought of the trauma of birth literally—that the experience was inevitably more or less traumatic in the physical sense and left its mark on the psyche in the form of primary anxiety. It was later that the physical separation of birth was replaced in his theory by the psychological importance of all separation experiences in the course of human life and that "birth" came to mean psychological birth—individuation.

Among the psychoanalysts of that time, and especially among members of the Committee, there existed, for many of the usual reasons, the inevitable professional rivalries for Freud's favor.[2] Yet this alone does not seem to account adequately for the hostility with which the book was received. There was something in the content of its message which touched deep levels of emotion in the psychology of those who first made contact with it. For, without Rank's awareness, it challenged not so much Freudian theory—into which it might, at least in part, have been absorbed—but the Freudian *Weltanschauung*, and thus the Freudian value system as it was reflected in therapy.

Essentially the Freudian view of man is of a creature condemned to inevitable conflict and suffering because of two opposing and largely irreconcilable needs: that for instinctual gratification, in the realms of sex and aggression, and that for socialization which dictates considerable deprivation of such gratifications. True, man can ameliorate the suffering through conscious understanding of himself and his situation, through sublimation of instinctual drives in work, and through gratification in mature love relationships. This view of the human situation is reflected in the Freudian philosophy of therapy which seeks, largely through the extension of consciousness (by making what was unconscious available to the ego), to provide the neurotic individual with the opportunity for new choices in his defensive and adaptive mechanisms.

Rank was unaware when he wrote *The Trauma of Birth* that he had embarked upon a very different voyage. He thought that his contribution would simply extend psychoanalytic understanding and, because of his profound identification with Freud and Freud's need, he hoped to provide the *nuclear* explanation for the existence of neurosis. In this Rank shared Freud's wish for the philosopher's stone. He wished to give it to Freud as a gift, and to this end dedicated *The Trauma of Birth* to Freud and most significantly presented it to him as a *birthday* present. Perhaps it is an old, Freudian habit of thought that causes me at this point to pay attention to the detail of content in trying to understand Rank's conflicted motivation. For example, the secrecy with which he prepared the work and his failure to inform the Committee concerning it, despite previous agreement among the Committee members that they would keep each other informed about their individual projects, was not only the result of the individually inspired character of his book (Taft's explanation) but reflected on the emotional intimacy which he felt for Freud and his need to keep it private. If, indeed, as the Freudians might say, this wish was an expression of unconscious, latent homosexual impulses, they were normally and most successfully and creatively sublimated, and in no way indicated the existence of the pathology of which Rank was accused.

But Rank's love for the father and his wish to express it by his gift, was counterbalanced by his unconscious wish for the philosopher's stone for himself. *The Trauma of Birth* represented his own birth, his own independent creative endeavor, his own separation as an individual.

In his devotion to Freud, Rank had repressed the birth implications of his original work on creativity, *Der Künstler*. While the thesis in that early work is essentially Freudian, based on the theory of the sublimation of sexual impulses, the concern with creativity as such heralds Rank's later view of man as creator—creator of himself and of his cultural environment.

It is essentially on the issue of birth as creation that the *Weltanschauung* in Rank's theory as expressed in *The Trauma of Birth* differs from Freud's. He would not deny the defensive and adaptive functions of the ego in relating to reality, as Freud saw them, but he saw in the physical act of separation at birth the paradigm, first for anxiety and then for the human psychological process of growth toward individuation—a condition both wished for and feared. Thus the center of conflict was not the opposition between sexual or aggressive wish and social need, but between the wish for the oneness of the womb, with its lack of differentiation, and the driving growth toward separateness, uniqueness, and individuation of the ego. To be born means to be responsible for one's own separate existence and survival; and in this separateness man experiences his finiteness; he comes to know of death, to fear the loss of his hard-won individuality, and to perceive the connection between birth and death. How often have we heard from patients and others, in their moments of despair and unhappiness, the accusation against the mother: "I didn't ask to be born!" Yet the birth into life is also felt as a gift and an opportunity for fulfillment. For Rank, this duality is a basic existential fact of human life. It cannot be resolved, but it can be made acceptable both through a relationship with another individual whose love accepts one's own individuality and uniqueness, and through the expression of one's own creativity, through which a certain immortality is assured. Later, when Rank developed his theories independently of Freud, he built into his theory of creativity our struggle to defy the finitude given us through birth, and to immortalize ourselves through some creative activity and product. But the seeds of these theories were already sown in *The Trauma of Birth* without his full awareness and they were, to my mind, unconsciously perceived by Freud and his followers, and were responsible for the severe criticism with which the book was received.

This gift to Freud carried a double message, just as any birth is at one and the same time a statement of separation and individuation, and of relatedness and belongingness. Rank's identification with Freud was profound, but in expressing it in the creative act of writing *The Trauma of Birth*, in his own reaching for individuality and immortality, he mirrored Freud's own overwhelming drive in this direction. This was at once a compliment and a threat—a compliment because it reflected Rank's deep attachment to Freud and his use of him as a model; a threat, not merely because the content of his new contribution challenged some of Freud's findings, but because Rank's own ambition for immortality and the inevitable guilt attendant thereon—a problem Rank understood and dealt with later in his career—reflected Freud's own needs and guilt. It is significant that the dual message in this fateful gift resulted in an ambivalent response on Freud's part. At first he received the work with pleasure. However, he had some doubts about its theoretical validity, especially in regard to an actual correlation between the difficulty of birth in an individual case and the degree of subsequent anxiety. He also had serious questions about the technical applicability of the birth trauma theory to shortening the length of treatment. By focusing on the analysis of this trauma itself, Freud nevertheless saw it as a contribution to psychoanalytic theorizing, especially in its attempt to find a paradigm for anxiety. It was Freud's followers, especially Jones and Abraham, who perceived *The Trauma of Birth* as a threat to the core of the theory of neurosis, namely to the concept of the castration complex, as well as a challenge to the whole of libido theory. They alerted Freud to what in their eyes was a danger to the entire structure of psychoanalytic theory and to the unity and cohesiveness of the psychoanalytic movement. Yet in the literature of psychoanalysis of that period, and certainly in the times that followed Rank's departure from the movement, there is practically no attempt to deal objectively with the actual content of Rank's new work, to evaluate it either positively or negatively in relationship to the specifics of psychoanalytic theory. Out of a mixture of envy and rivalry, fear and misunderstanding, ambivalence and conflict, *The Trauma of Birth* was dismissed out of hand.

What is the actual content of this controversial work? Rank, good Freudian clinician that he was, noted carefully the actual words in which patients expressed their emotions and attributed special meaning to this selective verbal choice. He tells us that in working with patients he noticed that in the end-phase of the analyses, when patients felt they were improving, they expressed feelings in terms of birth symbolism. Patients felt reborn or newborn, considering themselves the spiritual child of the analyst. While such an observation seems obvious, even trite, Rank was struck by an opposing duality in the expressed emotion: on the one hand, the infantility of the fantasy of rebirth (with its implication of a mother–child attachment to the analyst), on the other hand, borrowing a term from Jung, its "anagogic" character, namely the *striving* nature of birth itself—i.e., to exist and develop separately from the mother.

Rank puzzled about what he called "the *real* basis of thoughts of this kind." It would seem that by "real" Rank meant the biologic basis for the conflictful psychological feelings and thoughts surrounding the idea of birth. It is worth noting that the concern with harmonizing biological with psychological experience—in other words, with psychophysiology—was a Freudian preoccupation, and that in *The Trauma of Birth*, in this gift to Freud, Rank followed the same pattern of thought. He was searching for the fundamental, biological paradigm for anxiety, for the human attempts to master anxiety as expressed in culture, and for the failure of these attempts as expressed in the neuroses. On the basis of his observation that patients have great difficulty in separating from the analyst he came to the conclusion that "the strongest resistance to the severance of the libido transference at the end of the analysis is expressed in the form of the earliest infantile *fixation on the mother*." And then further:

the fixation on the mother, which seems to be at the bottom of the analytic fixation (transference), includes the earliest physiological relation to the mother's womb. . . . The patient's 're-birth phantasy' is simply a repetition in the analysis of his own birth. The freeing of the libido from its object, the analyst, seems to correspond to an *exact reproduction* of the first separation from the first libido object, namely of the new-born child from the mother.

Since the transference phenomenon in Rank's view is fundamentally a repetition of the child's attachment to the mother,

the work of the analysis, the solving and freeing of the libido 'neurotically' fixed on the analyst, is really neither more nor less than allowing the patient to repeat with better success in analysis the separation from the mother. But this, is by no means to be taken metaphorically in any way—not even in the psychological sense. . . . The patient repeats, biologically, as it were, the period of pregnancy—the reseparation from the substitute object. . . . *The analysis finally turns out to be a belated accomplishment of the incompleted mastery of the birth trauma.*[3]

At this point in the development of Rank's thinking we cannot but have conflicting feelings. In the light of modern knowledge about the importance of the early mother–child relationship for the future development of the individual, from Harlow's studies of attachment behavior in monkeys, to the most recent work of Bowlby, Winnicott, Mahler, and others, we must realize and acknowledge the pioneering nature of Rank's profound insight. *He was the first to shift the emphasis in the psychoanalytic understanding of human development from the male-oriented, Oedipal situation of childhood, with its ensuing castration anxiety as the center of conflict, to the initial mother-child relationship.* In doing this he opened the way to an ego psychology, since many of the current problems of identity, with which we make frequent clinical contact with our patients, and about which much has been written, hark back to struggles and conflicts surrounding separation from the mother and the formation of an autonomous, delimited, and relatively independent ego.

It is when Rank insists on the biological reality of the repeated separation from the mother, as it takes place in the analysis, as mother transference to the analyst, and eschews a metaphorical interpretation of these phenomena that we cannot agree with him.[4] For are not all psychological experiences of re-evoked emotion, which are touched off by memory images, to be understood metaphorically?

In a profound study of human psychology, Susanne Langer points to the difference between what she calls "practical" and "metaphorical" meaning in language and rote, and sees metaphor as the inevitable by-product of the nature of mind.[5] Indeed, since our experiences, both those deriving from contact with the outer world and those from our inner life, are preserved in the mind as memory images, the recall of these experiences and the accompanying emotion are analogous to the original. In this sense they are metaphorical. The memory is symbolized in the mind and may reappear, with its accompanying emotion, when there is a new reality, because its pattern, which resembles the situation of the original experience, re-evokes it. The new experience is "real" in its own right, but it is metaphorical in relation to the original experience it re-sembles. This difference is of critical importance in understanding the psychoanalytic process, especially in differentiating the transference from the "real" relationship and interaction between patient and analyst.

It would seem that Rank, in calling the separation of patient from analyst, i.e., the mother transference, a repetition of a *biological* reality, fails to account for this difference. He disregards the very metaphorical character of psychological repetition itself. This error is a continuation of the Freudian preoccupation with the search for a biological paradigm for psychological phenomena, and in this case Rank applied the paradigm to a psychological experience in the transference.

There is confusion in the Freudian theory of personality development on just such issues. For example, when Freud describes the Oedipus complex, he does so in the language of adult emotion, extrapolating from adult experience and projecting this experience backwards onto a developmental phase of childhood. In the therapeutic experience this phase is relived in the transference, but at no point does Freud make it clear that the transference experience, while having emotional reality of its own, is a metaphor in relation to the historical development of the individual. It is *analogous* to the original experience. In terms of Freudian theory, we would have to conclude that it is the discharge, the abreaction of the analogous emotions in the transference, that reduces the buildup of tensions due to the repression of the original traumatic experience. And indeed, Freud views the therapeutic effect of analysis as deriving in large measure from the possibility, created through the making-conscious of the repressed impulses and emotions, of mastery for the patient of the original, massive quantity of affect through its discharge in the experience of the transference. The emphasis in this conception of therapy is on the economic aspect of personality functioning—that is, on the discharge and distribution of instinct energy quantities: a process designed to serve the principle of constancy, to keep the organism in constant energic balance.

In *The Trauma of Birth* Rank holds an essentially similar view in economic terms. The universal experience of birth is considered traumatic in that the infant when transposed from the environment of the womb to the outside world, is flooded with excitation it cannot master. The resulting anxiety serves either to produce a fixation on the wish to return to the mother, in which case the individual becomes neurotic, or to propel him into future-directed, creative productivity. In both cases the issue is the overcoming of massive anxiety. Rank thought that an important factor in determining the quantity of initial anxiety was the actual nature of the birth experience. A difficult birth would create more anxiety than an easy one.

The help psychoanalysis can offer to the neurotic individual is, in Rank's terms, while he still thought of himself as a psychoanalyst, the re-creation in the transference experience of the original birth trauma of separation, which the patient is able to master because the relationship is a surrogate one, in which his adult ego has the opportunity, as he separates from the analyst, of identifying with the analyst's attitude toward the unconscious and of taking him as an ego-ideal. "The patient must learn in the course of the analysis so far to solve the primal repression, clinging to the mother, through 'transference' that he is able to transfer it to a real substitute object, without taking with it the primal repression."[6] In this reeducative task of detaching the libido from the mother fixation "we appeal to his conscious Ego," which is strengthened through making conscious his unconscious regressive tendencies." That his ego is in the position, through identification with the analyst, to overcome in the transference these actual libidinal tendencies as well as the regressive maternal tendencies can be explained from the fact that his Ego from the very beginning was created and developed from the Unconscious for this special task."[7]

It is ironic that *The Trauma of Birth*, which contains the seeds of deviation from the Freudian conception of personality and of therapy, and which marked the break between Rank and Freud, should (in part at least) be so Freudian in its adherence to an energic model of personality development, and to the therapeutic importance of repetition in the transference. Yet, despite this seeming irony, which grows out of Rank's historic roots, his understanding of ego processes, as these derive from object relations—for, indeed, birth itself bespeaks an interaction between two organisms—heralds the work of contemporary psychoanalysts like Kohut and Kernberg who, in their studies of narcissism, have refined our understanding of the subtleties of ego structure and processes as they have taken place in the developmental history of an individual and are reflected in the transference phenomena of the analytic situation. What Rank terms the "regressive maternal tendencies" of the patient comes close to Kernberg's concept of pathological narcissism and to Kohut's mirroring and idealizing transference. And for them, as well as for Rank, the therapeutic agent for the overcoming of these regressive, narcissistic fixations is, in addition to making these processes conscious in the transference, the identification with the analyst.

The anxiety induced by all the symbols of separation which echo the original separation of birth is illustrated by the dream of a young woman patient of mine which followed the move of her family into a newly purchased house:

"We move into our new house; it is terrible; the back yard, instead of being beautiful, is a graveyard containing the graves of all the previous owners. Also, there is a slum close by."

On one level the dream reflects the perfectionism of her extremely obsessive-compulsive character structure. She is always on the look-out for "the best" and is never sure that what she has is just that. In a state of doubting and uncertainty she is always looking for something better, be it a house, a job, furniture, or a dress. Her dream expresses the fear that the house may not be the best (which also includes the concept of the most advantageously priced) and failing this may be terrible. In her personal relationships she is highly ambivalent. In critical moments she asks herself: "Is my husband 'the best' I could have had?" "Does my only child meet my standards of perfection and reflect favorably upon me as a mother?" Her narcissism represents an identification with her own mother's extremely narcissistic relationship to her—a relationship in which her mother's demands expressed the older woman's need for a perfect daughter to reflect favorably upon her mothering and to outstrip her sisters, with whom she had a highly competitive relationship that expressed itself in constant comparisons between their daughters and her own. My patient has internalized her mother's image of her and has remained in a symbiotic relationship to her mother. Perhaps this symbiosis is represented by the graveyard in the back yard of the house and stands for the fact that she is haunted by her forebears, and fears that she cannot break away from her past.

It is the separation from this internalized narcissistic image that is the crucial therapeutic problem and it is at this point that Rank's profound insight into the issue of separation from the mother—i.e., birth as an individual—is crucial.[8]

My patient's dream expresses the fear of separation and individuation. To decide on a new house and to move into it carries a twofold implication. The house is a womb and moving into it is a return to the mother. But it is also a symbol of being grownup, of having a house of one's own. In this sense it means being born as a separate person. But to finalize something, especially to decide on a house, is to decide to *live* as well as to *die* there, for to live as an individual implies an awareness of life's finitude, and therefore involves the knowledge and fear of death. The theme of death is expressed in my patient's dream, through the image of the back yard (which in reality is very beautiful) as a graveyard in which all the previous owners of the house are buried.

The anxiety implicit in the process of birth itself is transformed through the emergence of consciousness from anxiety on a biological level, to psychological anxiety which is induced by all the symbols of separation and aloneness. With growing consciousness, the human creature gradually acquires an awareness of time, of growth and maturation, of age, and ultimately of death. Today we know that the problem of separation is much more than differentiation from the actual physical object of one's emotional investment—originally the mother. It is even more than the evocation of separation anxiety by the symbols for the primal separation. It is, in the course of maturation, separation from the unconscious *internalization* of the primal love object—from all the images, attitudes, emotions, and memories which the childhood experiences in the interaction with the mother had created. Although Rank saw the importance of processes of internalization, it was primarily in relation to the therapeutic task of overcoming the birth trauma that he speaks of identification with the analyst.[9] In *The Trauma of Birth* he was interested in the biological basis of the psychological, primarily in the overcoming of anxiety: therapeutically through identification, socially and historically through the creation of culture in all its aspects—myth, art, religion, ritual, and social mores.

In understanding Rank it is important to realize that he himself was in the process of evolving. At the time of the writing of *The Trauma of Birth*, he was still firmly influenced by certain fundamental Freudian concepts. For example, the very use of the term "trauma" in connection with birth relates it to an energic phenomenon. The infant must assimilate a large amount of stimulation to which the birth experience subjected it. This stimulation must, therefore, somehow be discharged or assimilated. In some individuals the abreaction was incomplete, and Rank saw this as the root of neurotic difficulties. His conception of the analytic task, therefore, was to provide an opportunity for this abreaction of the birth trauma in the transference.

The fixation on the mother is at the bottom of the transference resistance, for the patient wishes to re-create the original mother–child relationship which preceded the act of birth: in other words, to return to the womb. Herein lies another important link of Rank's thinking to the Freudian system of thought from which he emerged—the concept of regression. The human wish to return to the primal pleasure of the intrauterine experience as a basic source of human motivation is reminiscent of Freud's *Beyond the Pleasure Principle*, in which he emphasized the regressive tendency of all living creatures: that is, ultimately to return to the original inanimate state from which all life emerged. It is from this conception of life's backward movement that Freud derived the death instinct, and it is of interest that at the point in his career when Rank wrote *The Trauma of Birth*, he advanced a regressive theory of motivation which led him to the womb—a point at which in the undifferentiation of the individual, birth and death meet.

Perhaps both men, who were influenced in the derivation of their theories by clinical experience, were constantly impressed by the extent of human passive wishes. Only Rank, however, saw clearly that the analytic situation itself stimulated such wishes. "Above all, the analytic situation, which historically has developed from the hypnotic state, seems to challenge a direct comparison between the Unconscious and the primal state."[10]

From the beginning of his concern with the human situation, Rank was impressed by man's creative striving, but initially he saw all the products of culture as a compromise between the wish to reunite with the mother and an adaptation to the reality of separateness. In this conception of compromise in the motivation toward creativity, the regressive element predominated. This was his view at the time of the writing of *The Trauma of Birth*. At this time Rank was averse to the notion of "striving," for he wrote critically of Jung's conception of rebirth as having an ethical-anagogic element—anagogic referring to striving. He saw it as too psychological and insufficiently biological. We shall have occasion later on to trace a change in his thinking from the more regressive view of human motivation to an understanding of man's need to give meaning to his life and to ensure his immortality by *merging* (through a personally created product or identification) with some element (be it an individual, a cosmic idea, or an ideology) that is larger and more powerful than himself.[11]

At this point, the more regressive notion of the wish to return to the womb evolves into a conception of creative striving for perpetuity. The meeting point of both views is Rank's awareness of the burdensome nature of separateness and of individuation, and of the anxiety it produces—an anxiety that can best be mastered by transforming it into an affirmation of the growth principle and a view of life as an opportunity for creative mastery. It is in *The Trauma of Birth* that Rank begins the odyssey of this profound understanding.

In conclusion, we should ask: What placed this pioneering work in such jeopardy that its contributions were overlooked and that its title became solely a disdainful byword with which Rank's name was only too often identified. There are aspects of the work which militated against it (aside from the tensions it precipitated within the psychoanalytic movement stemming largely from reasons of personal rivalry and envy) that finally resulted in its dismissal. The title itself is unfortunate, for it harks back to Freud's already abandoned traumatic theory of the neuroses and represents Rank's attempt to stay within the psychoanalytic system of thought. In insisting on the biological reality of the birth trauma and the need to assimilate and overcome it as the single driving force behind all our personal and cultural achievements, Rank extended his view of the causality of motivation beyond reasonable proportions: oversimplifying and overgeneralizing it at the same time.

Formally, his use of the birth trauma parallels Freud's extended view of sexuality and of the sexual drives as the prime mover in human development, experience, and creativity. Furthermore, the birth trauma theory was a challenge to the primacy of Freud's theory of sexual drives. Rank attempted to reconcile the two views of motivation by conceiving of castration anxiety as a later phase of birth anxiety.[12] However, the two views of the driving force for human behavior are of a different order. Freud's is indeed an instinct theory. But what instinct would lead us to be motivated throughout our individual lives, in fact throughout human history, by the need to abreact the fear precipitated by the birth experience? In such a view, anxiety—an ego phenomenon—is at the center of the theory. Although Rank was not fully aware of this, it is precisely this introduction of the ego function as the central concept in human motivation that became both the contribution of Rank's theory and the point at which it was incompatible with Freudian theory.

Had Rank not eschewed a metaphorical understanding of the birth experience in all the symbolic and psychological forms of separation and individuation which it acquires in the course of a lifetime, his theory might have found acceptance. For, during the half century which has followed Rank's work, in the writings of Klein, Winnicott, Mahler, the issue of the mother–child relationship and of the separation between them as crucial for human development has become of paramount importance.

The Trauma of Birth was further jeopardized by Rank's attempt to explain the neuroses on the basis of the extent and degree of the actual trauma experienced by the individual at birth. Again his literal insistence on the physical experience diverted him from its symbolic, psychological meaning and greatly oversimplified the theory of the genesis of neurosis. He hoped to apply this oversimplified theory to the treatment of the neuroses by focusing the analysis primarily on the derivations of the birth trauma experience as they appeared in the transference. In this way he sought to shorten the analytic procedure by setting a terminal date as a way of reproducing the experience of separation from the mother. However, it should be noted that, as described in *The Trauma of Birth*, Rank's prescribed technique is first the "overcoming [of] the primal resistance, namely the mother–fixation, with regard to his [the analyst's] own person in the transference relation, *then* a definite term is fixed for the analysis."[13]

Regardless of the limitation and constricting effect of all prescribed techniques of therapy and therefore of Rank's approach as well, the introduction of the issue of separation and individuation within the framework of the mother–child relationship, as it is relived in the transference, must be viewed as an early, major, and much overlooked contribution to the meaning of therapy. But *The Trauma of Birth* initiated a contribution destined to have even more far-reaching import: Rank began to see that the overcoming of primal anxiety, which he identified as birth fear, could take two very different routes: one in the direction of neurotic symptom and character formation, the other in the direction of creative productivity. While the birth trauma as a primary causal explanation for the genesis of neurosis is extravagantly oversimplified, the direction to which it points, the issue of separation from the mother, has useful clinical applicability. I shall illustrate this later.

When the wish to return to the mother as a way of mastering anxiety is expressed creatively, either as a merging of oneself with some higher ideal or in the projection of a part of the self into a product that will outlive the self—a point at which the wish for oneness with the mother and the wish for immortality meet—we are confronted with a new theory of creativity. Although at this point in his development Rank still used Freudian terminology and speaks of sublimation, he was in effect advancing an ego theory of motivation for which the term sublimation, which refers to changing the aim of an instinctual drive, is no longer applicable.

The Trauma of Birth marks a turning point and a waystation in Rank's career. It is the creative expression of his own rebirth—of his struggle to become autonomous and yet to belong to the psychoanalytic family. This accounts for its exaggerations and its contradictions. Yet these should not blind us to its contributions, nor to the fact that it contains the seeds of even more profound insights.

SEVEN

On Fear and Anxiety

A S WE HAVE just seen, Rank's theory of anxiety was initially wedded to two fundamentally Freudian concerns: the role of trauma in precipitating anxiety and the hope of finding a prototype for anxiety—one that would explain all future anxieties in the life of an individual as well as the origin of neurosis. The emphasis on trauma came from the psychophysical orientation in the psychological science of that time, which saw the human organism as primarily concerned with keeping its equilibrium in the face of exposure to a great deal of excitation. The focus on anxiety derived for both men from its prevalence in the neurotic patients whom they sought to treat. For Freud, whose emphasis was on sexual etiology, the prototype for anxiety and the cure of neurosis was castration anxiety; for Rank early in his career it was the birth experience.

Fear is an inevitable accompaniment of life for all living organisms: it constitutes an essential part of an instinctual survival mechanism. As I have noted elsewhere: "The important fact is that fear is a universal response of living tissue, whether manifested in the simple avoidance response of the stentor when an irritant is introduced into its environment or transformed through the evolution of the higher brain centers into a consciously experienced awareness of anxiety in man."[1] Fear is transformed into anxiety through the advent of conscious awareness, most especially of self-awareness. Thus the precursor of anxiety viewed biologically is raw fear itself, but since one can scarcely speak of awareness in the newborn infant, birth trauma does not appear to be the cause of anxiety. That some impressions of the experience may be imprinted upon the nervous system is plausible, but that a theory of anxiety, much less a causal theory of neurosis, may be based upon the nature and severity of the birth experience seems scarcely credible. Rank himself realized this and gave up the literal interpretation of anxiety as deriving from the separation of mother and child in the birth experience to adhere to a metaphorical interpretation of this separation. Not physical separation of the two, but their psychological separation as it takes place through the development of individuation now became the paradigm for anxiety. The significance of this step from the psychophysical to the purely psychological can scarcely be overestimated. It marks the beginning of a true ego psychology more than fifty years before our current concern with issues of separation and individuation.[2]

In the course of the child's normal growth and development, the unfolding of given potentialities supports the process by which autonomy is achieved. This includes the mastery of bodily functions, of the physical environment, of intellectual activity, and of human relationships. But human development is never simply the unfolding of inherent capacities. Each step in growth is fueled by the developing will of the individual with accompanying affect and takes place within a social framework—initially the dyad of mother and child. The experience of growth is never a completely positive one: The extreme dependency of the human child is prolonged; emotions are generated in the interpersonal interactions during development, and one is aware of them as well as of the deeper, less conscious imprints they leave. Fundamentally growth connotes separation and therefore produces fear and subsequently anxiety. One has but to observe the first steps of a one year old child who is just about to raise himself to the upright position to see reflected on his face a mixture of determination and will, anxiety and dismay, vying with glee. In growing the child is separating not only from the mother physically and psychologically, but from a part of his own past experience—an experience in which he was less differentiated as a separate person than in the ensuing phase of development. Rank writes: "In the psychic separation experience as it is represented in the development of individuality through the giving up of outlived parts of one's own past, we have to recognize an individualistic expression of the biological principle of growth."[3]

It is the uncertainty in a changing situation which produces fear and anxiety. For the child learning to walk there are the unformulated but implied feelings of anxiety which we might state as follows: will I be able to master the task; does my need and wish to do so override my capacity; will I fall; will my mother protect me if I do; will she be pleased and happy about my achievement, or experience it as my leaving her, a rejection? Obviously the infant child does not think these things in this form, but the emotions surrounding the issue of growing away from the mother are felt in ways for which we have only our adult conceptualizations. Our justification for such retrospective speculation lies in the observation of adults who have not taken their first steps toward autonomy successfully and whose failure can be traced, at least in part, to inhibiting experiences in early childhood. A patient I have discussed elsewhere[4] comes to mind, because the deficits in her adult sense of self can be traced to many aspects of early interaction with her mother, and also quite literally to her first steps. Her mother's hostile rejection of her child resulted, among other things, in great anxiety for the child's life and welfare at every step in development. When the little girl was old enough to walk the mother, fearing injury, prevented this normal development by wheeling her around in a carriage. Needless to say, the child herself absorbed the fear, and it was not until she was three years of age that the mother, under the critical pressure of friends and relatives, took her to a kind of witch doctor who, by uttering some magical incantations, allayed the little girl's fears, and succeeded in getting her to walk. The mother's fear of and lack of support for succeeding phases of growth was reflected throughout my patient's life in her own anxiety, her phobic reactions, her overcompliance, and her low self-esteem.

The normal process of separation and the establishment of phase-appropriate autonomy was interfered with by the mother's anxiety, which was communicated to the child, and by the mother's failure to affirm the growth processes. This little girl would have needed an unimaginable effort of will to transcend her mother's fears, to resist the contamination by anxiety, to assert her own needs and wishes, and thus to effect a psychological separation from her mother.

Rank was keenly aware of the importance of the nature of the early mother–child relationship and of its bearing upon the outcome of the separation process. Yet no matter how felicitous this relationship, separation invariably leads to anxiety. It is the human will, riding the wave of maturation and change, which insists on the individual's right and need to be autonomous, differentiated, and separated from the maternal matrix. Thus the will and anxiety are inextricably connected. According to Rank, "The will to freedom can only be admitted timidly and gradually because it is denied on the one hand because of the emotional tie, (originally to the mother) and inhibited by fear on the other."[5]

The price for the exercise of will in the achievement of individuality is thus anxiety. But even when that price has been paid, the individual is not free of another fear: that of the loss of his dearly bought autonomy. From earliest childhood the emotional bonds of love so essential for the normal development of the self, can also become threatening when they beckon to one's wish to remain one with the object of love, and to avoid the anxiety of separation. The anxiety of separation is matched by the anxiety of merging, and both are fueled by counterbalancing wishes.

In the overwhelming wish and will to grow, separation from the past is inevitable. Before conscious self-awareness is well developed, the fear engendered by separation, originally from the mother, stems from the uncertainty as to whether the growing self can successfully sustain its integrity in the transition between one phase of development and the next. Fear is thus an indicator of the cohesiveness of the self, of the strength of the will, and of the individual's ability to persist in implementing it. But this unavoidable fear is generated not solely from the unfolding of developmental processes within the individual, but by the complicating fact that for the human being development takes place within a social context in which the bonds of attachment must be partially severed in the process of separation and individuation. According to Rank, such severing of ties is experienced by the growing child—and sometimes by the mother as well—as a hostile, rejecting act. Therefore the fear of total loss of the mother's love as retribution for hostility augments the fear which originates from the separation implicit in growth itself.

The growing child depends on the mother's love and affirmation as nourishment for the normal development of the self. The very self which strives for independence also needs to preserve a goodly measure of

dependency—a dependency which changes its character to a mature relatedness as life proceeds. The need to ensure the continuity of such
nourishment accounts for the fact that the threat of loss and the ensuing
fear can give rise to the wish to return to the mother—to merge with
her.

Thus the developing individual moves through life between two fears:
the fear of differentiation through separation and individuation and the
fear of merging through union and symbiosis. Stated another way, the
individual fears both the becoming of a self, and the dissolution of that
very self. From Rank's own words one can see how far he has come
from the search for a single prototype for fear and the literal interpretation
of fear as the result of the traumatic experience of birth.

> The fear in birth, which we have designated as fear of life, seems to me
> actually the fear of having to live as an isolated individual, and not the
> reverse, the fear of the loss of individuality (death fear). That would mean,
> however, that primary fear corresponds to a fear of separation from the
> whole, therefore a fear of individuation, on account of which I should like
> to call it fear of life, although it may appear later as fear of the loss of this
> dearly bought individuality, as fear of death, of being dissolved again into
> the whole. Between these two fear possibilities, these poles of fear, the
> individual is thrown back and forth all his life, which accounts for the fact
> that we have not been able to trace fear back to a single root, or to overcome
> it therapeutically.[6]

As self-awareness increases in the course of growing up, the consciousness of death becomes part of the psychic life. Here again we are
confronted by a duality in regard to fear for the self: the fear of separating
from all that has formed and supported the self in terms of human
relationships, worldly satisfaction, and achievement, and the fear of a
dissolution and disappearance of the self into a cosmic whole. The common denominator in the psychology of fear is loss, be it of the love-
object or of the self.

In the face of this two-pronged existential fear Rank addresses the
question of how the human being copes with the inevitability of loss.
The solution, to the extent one can call it that, (it is only an amelioration
of the fear), resides in the creative impulse which at different levels of
development and in two varying ways strives for immortality. The creation of progeny allays the fear of extinction of the self. It is the biological

solution to the wish for immortality. In addition, for many, identification with and participation in some communal endeavor—be it religious, political, or cultural—represents an opportunity to perpetuate the self as part of a larger whole which will outlive the mortal self. The highly individualized personality, however, must seek its own immortality and must try to subdue fear through its own creative efforts. This is especially true of the creative artist, as I have noted earlier (chapters 3 and 4).

It is in the attempt to understand and cope with our primal fear that psychology and philosophy come together. Rank was not unmindful of the tragic nature of human life. On the contrary, he saw in the dilemma of a creature who had acquired conscious awareness and a sense of self, yet was called upon through the finitude of life to relinquish that very self, the tragic element in human existence. Nevertheless, his panoramic knowledge of human history, religion, mythology, and literature enabled him to reach beyond the psychology of the individual or of the group— even beyond psychology itself—and to perceive our capacity to transcend our fear. This optimistic emphasis in Rank's thinking is based on his awareness of the indomitable thrust of the life force. If we joined it in a creative expression of our own, we could in some measure master the reality of our mortality. "Man is born beyond psychology and he dies beyond it but he can *live* beyond it only through vital experience of his own—in religious terms, through revelation, conversion or re-birth."[7] This statement is not a call for a specific religious or mystical experience. Rather, it is a celebration of the spiritual capacity of the creative will to deal with the bitter reality of its own end by identifying with the continuity of life itself. According to Rank it is the will to live rather than the fear of death which spurs the creative impulse to reach for immortality. While at first glance it may seem that there is little difference between the will to live and the fear of death, the difference in emphasis is crucial. It changes Rank's philosophy of life, his view of neurosis and of the therapeutic endeavor from what might have been a narrow and pessimistic resignation to the finitude of the life of the self, to an optimistic—yet realistic—appraisal of the creative potentialities inherent in man, which make possible an overcoming of fear and a generating of a bid for immortality. According to Rank, neurosis is an insufficiency of the creative impulse toward self-realization because it is inhibited by the fear of separation—ultimately of loss through death.

The therapeutic endeavor, therefore, must deal primarily with this fear, its major vehicle being the relationship to the therapist. It is Rank's faith in the possibility of transcending fear and anxiety by freeing the creative forces within the individual that informs his therapeutic approach. It was a unique point of view at the time of his writing; it is one which is applicable today. We shall have more to say in detail about Rank's therapeutic philosophy later.

EIGHT

The Social Dimension

HUMAN BEINGS, experiencing two great anxieties—that of their own individuated growth and that of the loss of their dearly bought selves—strive for perpetuation through the expression of their creative will. This may be expressed in a product of their own individual efforts or in an identification with social values as these are manifested in religious, aesthetic, political, or even scientific ideologies. Rank was keenly aware that the process by which we move through time is a ceaseless interaction of living forces: those of our own development and differentiation with those of social change. Society itself, like a living organism, responds creatively to the forces of environmental change. Such change may stem from causes as diverse as geographic upheaval, cataclysmic historical events, the psychological impact of new scientific and technological discoveries, or the moral influence of an outstanding leader. For example, in describing cultural change in the society of the Manus peoples of the Admiralty Islands, as it expressed itself in "The Paliau Movement," Margaret Mead[1] considers the unit of change the cultural contribution of an exceptional individual (Paliau) who influenced a group or "cluster" of significant individuals to help bring about a social program that called for a widening of the sphere of human sympathy and a diminution therefore of near-neighbor antagonisms, an almost complete abandonment of old traditions, and long-time planning and saving for the future in order to build a new way of life.[2] This example makes clear how an outstanding individual leader can effect social progress; but whatever the cause, social and cultural change is continuous, although certainly at differing rates in particular societies. It brings along change in social institutions, in values, and in *Weltanschauung*. It is in the realm of values that society has the greatest impact on the development of the individual.

Before the advent of Rank, and to some extent even today, psychoanalysis considered its findings "scientific" and therefore outside the realm of values.[3] It failed to see that even the most objective findings of the "hard sciences"—for example the discovery of atomic fission—inevitably impinge upon social values, challenging their traditional position and calling for change. It was also unaware that its generalizations, which derived from a study of the individual without regard for the social framework in which he lived, led to psychological absolutism inimical to the purported goals of scientific truth for which psychoanalysis itself supposedly stood. Thus for example the Oedipus complex, the psychoanalytic psychology of women, and the conception of norms for sexual and social behavior are not universals in their content but are relative to the structures and values of the social milieu from which they derive. It was Rank who understood and emphasized this relativity. What he saw as universal was the *interactional process* between individual growth and social experience which led to continuous change.

As we have already indicated (chapter 3), in his earliest work, *Der Künstler*, Rank was aware of the interaction between the artist and the society. The artist's sublimated work of art, which expressed needs of his own (and at that time Rank still spoke in Freudian terms), spoke to similar needs in the people of his time. In this sense there is congruity between the striving of the individual for self-realization and the social need to share in this individual expression, thus vicariously experiencing a portion of the artist's creativity. Yet society, as a collective, an aggregate of individuals, represents and expects a certain conformity in the name of the perpetuation of its traditions. To some extent, therefore, the process of individuation is inevitably in conflict with the demands for conformity. The ceaseless interaction between the individual and the social milieu results in a relationship characterized by both congruence and conflict. Historically this is manifested in periodic shifts in the ascendancy either of collectivism or individualism. When the former is paramount the individual succumbs to the equalizing and leveling forces of the social environment. When individualism is uppermost, the exceptional individual, tending toward differentiation from the mass, becomes the vehicle for change much as a genetic mutation becomes the instrument of biological change.[4]

Thus conformity and differentiation exist as essential interacting forces in the maintenance and development of man's psycho-social life. But Rank emphasizes the fact that the dynamic relationship between them is a force of balance and not solely a source of conflict.

This view of the individual's relationship to society as a productive, dynamic interaction contrasts sharply with Freud's. He viewed society, with its prohibitions and expectations of conformity, as being in opposition to the development of the individual.[5] In Freud's view since individual development is dominated by the instinct life and is motivated first by the pleasure principle and only secondarily by the reality principle such opposition creates conflict for the individual. It is the nature of attempts to resolve this conflict which largely determines the psychological character of the individual.

Rank did not deny the existence of conflict for the human creature, but saw it *not* as primarily stemming from the opposition between the individual and society, but as residing in the very nature of the life process itself—a growth process in the course of which human self-awareness makes the knowledge of death inevitable. The task both for society and for the individual centers around the mastery of life's finitude.[6]

Whether in the striving for individuation or in the formation of the social collective in terms of tradition, values, beliefs, myths, or social institutions, the motivation is the same: the wish for immortality.

In the course of human development, the struggle with the fact of mortality experienced evolutionary changes. Early in human history, immortality was an individual and a very literal matter, for it referred to the belief in the survival of the bodily self. At this level it was purely individualistic, but with the development of the idea of the existence of a spiritual dimension in the world came the possibility of sharing with others a common belief under the social dominion of a spiritual system. The conception of the survival of an individual bodily self was transformed into a belief in individual spiritual immortality through participation in a collective soul. Thus, according to Rank, religion evolved and a powerful bond between the individual self and the social collective was formed out of the need to deal with the finiteness of human existence. The possibility for the individual of resolving this profound existential conflict through identification with a collective ideology exists today and is a major avenue for the discovery of meaningfulness in life. In *Psychology and the Soul*, Rank traced the evolution of the relationship of individualism and collectivism from the development of religion, through the formation of familial organization, to the emergence of the state and the legal solution of the problem of perpetuity through reproductive generation.[7]

It is the loss of oneness through individuation and awareness, be it the oneness with the maternal womb or with the unaware world of living things, that concerns Rank; for it is this which makes for the inevitability of human conflict and suffering. The attempts to ameliorate this suffering through religious beliefs or secular ideologies are neither pathological nor infantile, as Freud[8] would have it, but are, according to Rank, creative attempts to deal with conflict.

Closely linked to the creation of religious belief, yet in some ways in opposition to it, is artistic expression—a most important attempt to create perpetuity. Art, says Rank, "has an end . . . not concrete and practical . . . [but] abstract and spiritual."[9] In its beginnings art "was not the satisfaction of the desire of the individual artist to attain immortality for himself in his work, but the confirmation of the collective immortality—idea in the work itself as a picture of the soul." The idea represented in art is the concretization of the spiritual to prove its existence and to demonstrate its indestructibility. In this sense it is religious, and to the extent that the individual artist's work expresses the collective religious will, he is in tune with the social milieu of his time. Yet, as we have already made clear, the individual and society are in constant evolutionary movement. As a result, the two creative processes—those of the individual self and those of society—are not always synchronized. The creative artist is highly individuated; social change is determined by many variables which give rise to new and often unpredictable forms and ideologies. Thus a gap may arise between the creative expression of the individual and that of society.

Since religious ideology is collective, the creative work of the artist who strives for ever-clearer expression of his individuality may come in conflict with the cultural ideology of his time. Paradoxically, this may be true even if the artist uses the religious forms of his era for his individual expression. Rank puts it this way: "The development of art has always striven beyond religion. . . . this tendency toward independence corresponds to an irreligiousity . . . that is inherent and essential in all artistic creation. . . . Personal creativity is antireligious in the sense that it is always subservient to the individual desire for immortality in the creative personality and not to the collective glorification of the creator of the world . . . [the artist] tries to save his individuality from the collective mass by giving his work the stamp of his own personality."[10]

Rank obviously does not mean that an individual artist may not also be imbued with religious feeling, but that the artist's impulse toward creative expression is motivated largely by a desire to perpetuate himself. "Religion springs from the collective belief in immortality; art from the personal consciousness of the individual. The conflict between art and religion, which we can so easily trace in the individual artist, is thus ultimately a conflict between individuality and collectivity, the dualistic struggle within the creative artist of the two impulses of his own self."[11]

In all human beings the impulses of separation and differentiation conflict with merging and oneness. Rank sees the same conflict even in an interpretation of so collective a creation as the myth. There, the opposition between embeddedness and differentiation is reflected in the struggle of generations. In the myth of the hero,[12] the hostility of one generation to the next as a common denominator is expressed in the obstacles which surround the very birth of the hero, as if the father figure around whom major conflict centers actually attempted to prevent it. The victorious hero, however, overcomes all the obstacles, and emerges as a highly individuated figure with whom the general populace can identify. Rank draws an analogy between folk myths which attempt to portray the struggle of the future generation to break away from its antecedents, and the fantasies of the individual child striving for personal independence. These fantasies often take the form of the so-called "family romance"—an attempt to replace the actual parents by highly idealized imaginary ones. In asserting his difference and separation from the parents, "the ego of the child behaves in this respect like the hero of the myth."[13]

"The detachment of the growing individual from the authority of the parents is one of the most necessary, but also one of the most painful achievements of evolution. . . . Social progress is essentially based upon this opposition between the two generations."[14] In the creation of the myth we have a clear example of the support which a cultural manifestation can give the growing ego of an individual through the offer of an opportunity for emulation—emulation of the hero. Thus the relationship between the individual and society is not solely one of opposition or conflict, but also one of productive interaction in which needs on both sides can be met and reinforced.

Rank's thinking about life is imbued with the awareness of paradox and dichotomy. The tension created by such dualities is responsible for change and progress both in the individual and in society. But our need to *control* this movement toward change, which includes an understanding of ourselves, to feel that we are its major instrument, often becomes an obstacle to the positive outcome of our striving. This is because our attempts at mastery are overwhelmingly governed by the rational at the expense of the irrational. Since in our Western "scientific" culture we are prejudiced in favor of the rational, and in fact strive for its ascendency in most situations, it is not easy to understand what Rank means by this dichotomy and especially by his use of the term irrational.

By irrational he does not mean madness or insanity as the term is sometimes commonly used. According to Rank, life's forces by their very nature are fundamentally irrational in the sense that events can not always be causally explained, justified, mastered, controlled, or altered. Man, however, having acquired awareness and self-awareness through evolutionary processes, has overestimated the power of rational mind, assuming that its achievements, which are indeed importantly adaptive as well as magnificent, can be extended limitlessly. This attitude of omnipotence leads to a failure on the individual level to accept the nature of life and to deal creatively with its inevitabilities—especially with the fact of death.

On the social level the attempts to control the movements of the forces of life through absolutist explanations or ideologies lead in time to disillusionments which bring about social crisis and call for social change. But far from regarding with pessimism either the individual struggle to accept the irrationality of life or the social struggle to find new forms through which the individual can come into his own and yet achieve a sense of unity and oneness, Rank accepts these processes as inevitable. They represent the rational attempts of a self-aware, sentient creature whose psychological development requires great emotional nutriment to live within the framework of the irrational forces of life. As I have noted elsewhere: "In the constant movement of sociopsychological forces, the adaptive balance between man's psychology and behavior and the outer forces of the environment, be they physical or social, is constantly being challenged. According to Rank this balance is reconstituted by processes of evolution and revolution. These are not alternating but aspects of a larger ongoing process of continual change."[15]

However, it is important to remember that the life forces are not characterized solely by their deviation from a causal determinism—i.e., by irrationality—but also by the quality of striving. This becomes manifest in the creative expression of the individual will as well as in social change. It is in the interplay between individual creativity and the cultural ideologies and symbols of a particular time that psychosocial evolution advances.

Rank's keen awareness of the psychosocial process as it is reflected in mythology, artistic creativity, religion and secular ideologies, is nowhere more apparent than in his understanding of the relationship of the psychology of woman to that of man. In an article, "Feminine Psychology and Masculine Ideology," which reveals the extent to which he was ahead of his time, Rank deals with all these dimensions in probing the history of the development of the attitudes of one sex to the other.[16] By doing so, Rank illustrates in considerable detail the interaction of social forces upon individual psychology.

It is clear that, for a long time, both individually and collectively a masculine way of life has been imposed upon woman. Rank attributes this in large measure to man's attempt to blot out his mother-origin in order to deny his mortal nature. For to be born of woman is to share one's fate with all other living creatures whose birth inaugurates the inevitability of death. Mythology, religion, art, and social organization reflect the attempt through "an undifferentiated mixture of biological facts and supernatural ideologies"[17] to prove man's supernatural origins, and therefore his immortality. The myth of the self-created hero is an example of the creation of a masculine ideal which dominated ancient society by replacing the original mother-culture. The masculine ideal is also exemplified in the creation of a masculine state organization which has persisted, certainly in the Western world, until quite recently.

Rank postulates a fundamental difference in the nature of the will of the two sexes. Man's will expresses itself as "wanting," woman's in "wanting to be wanted." Woman's strength lies in her sex which is receptive; man's strength lies in his creative will. Man fears chaos; woman fears loss and separation. Man finds it hard to accept himself as mortal and rationalizes his sense of himself as independent of woman. Woman is closer to an acceptance of her basic self, which is tied to motherhood. Yet because she is imbued with masculine ideology, which dominates social standards and values, she needs constant confirmation from the man that she is acceptable to him.

These generalizations, manifested in some individualized form and varying in intensity, are familiar to all clinicians. Yet it is not clear in Rank's writing to what extent he regards the psychological differences between the sexes as inherent and to what extent he views them as products of social influences. Few of us today would agree that woman's inherent strength lies primarily in her sexual receptivity, or that man's lies in his creative will. We would view these differences as the result of societal values—differences which are becoming somewhat obscured by changes in norms and in social and sexual roles. But the importance of Rank's contribution lies not in an accurate appraisal of the origins of psychological differences between the sexes, but in that he acknowledged the interplay of social and psychological forces in creating the existing differences he affirms. Rank makes very clear that equality between the sexes—for that matter equality among peoples—does not mean the obliteration of differences, but rather the right of all of us to become and to be ourselves and to accept and be accepted *in our own differences*.

This affirmation of difference which sparks creativity informs all of Rank's thinking. It derives from his profound awareness of the relativity of norms as they evolve in the interactional process between the individual and his social environment, as that process both collectively and individually strives toward perpetuity. While this point of view derives from a deep understanding of psychosocial processes, it eventuates in a philosophical ethic which has important implications in its practical application to psychotherapeutic procedure. I shall show how the acceptance of difference on the part of the therapist facilitates the acceptance and development of self-delineation in the therapeutic process.

NINE

The Double

A Contribution to the Understanding of Narcissism

ONE MIGHT well ask whether the motif of the double in the writings of Otto Rank is merely a curiosity in the concerns of a man keenly observant, highly sensitive and limitlessly inquisitive or whether it has some important bearing on an understanding of human psychology and therefore ultimately on psychotherapeutic intervention. Rank, of course, was an avid reader of literature, mythology, and cultural history. In his intellectual odyssey he frequently encountered the theme of the double—in German the Doppelgänger—and was intrigued by it. He sensed its universality and its manysided social and psychological meaning and function. Therefore, Rank's insights into the meaning of this motif transcend mere curiosity and illuminate aspects of the development and nature of the self, of its relationship to existential issues, and of its interaction with society as a whole.

Before going into the details of Rank's interpretations of the double's various manifestations, it is important to grapple with the term itself. Double is inevitably an inadequate translation of Doppelgänger, which contains a somewhat mystical meaning. It is compounded with the German verb "to go" (literally, "double-goer"), and therefore implies a more active quality than the English noun "double" can convey. Throughout Rank's writings it has many meanings: for example, a protective or pursuing spirit, an alter-ego, or the immortal soul. In other words, in the term Doppelgänger, Rank found a generic term to cover the many meanings and manifestations of the double as it appears in mythology and literature. The understanding of these meanings which Rank dealt with in various writings throughout his life enriches our understanding of important aspects of the formation and nature of human identity.

The phenomenon of being able to project a double image attests to the creative human capacity to split off some part either of the existing self or of a wished-for self in an effort to maintain some integrity at the core of the self. To the extent that this projection is a self phenomenon it is an aspect of narcissism; to the extent that it serves to protect certain aspects of the self it is a defensive operation; and to the extent that it represents certain aspirations of the self and facilitates the consolidation and growth of the self it is part of a developmental process.

In *The Double* Rank begins, after calling attention to the frequent appearance in literature of the motif of the double, by a statement of the problem: namely "that a person's past inescapably clings to him and that it becomes his fate as soon as he tries to get rid of it."[1] The reference here is clearly to some undesirable aspect of the past or of a mark which this past has left on the nature of one's personality. It is through some form of projection or splitting off that the individual protagonist of the many tales Rank cites attempts to foil pursuit by his double self. The romantic literature Rank refers to is replete with countless examples of the individual's struggle with an alter-ego, most often represented as "the shadow" or "the mirror-image." In an introduction to his excellent translation of *The Double*, Tucker notes "It is not surprising . . . that the theme of the double prominently appeared just when introspective German Romanticism was nascent," since "The quest into the mind is simultaneously the quest into the individuality and integrity of the self."[2]

The link with romanticism is clear in the examples Rank mentions. "The classical creator of the double-projection" in German literature is E. T. A. Hoffman, who became the model and inspiration for future works, as for example Heinz Ewers' *The Student of Prague*, or Chamisso's *Peter Schlemihl*, or Jean Paul's *Siebenkas* or *Titan*. These writings are not as familiar to the English reader as Oscar Wilde's *Picture of Dorian Gray* or Edgar Allan Poe's *William Wilson*, which Rank also cites. But for a detailed account of how the authors develop the theme of self-projection through plot and character delineation the reader must turn to Rank's original work.

Sometimes the split-off part of the self represents both the abhorred and idealized aspect of the self-image, in addition to the conscience as in *Dorian Gray*; or it is clearly the super-ego as in Poe's *William Wilson*. In de Mauppassant's *The Horla*, the central character is possessed by an invisible spirit, the product of his fear of aloneness, which watches him, controls him, and pursues him, while in Dostoyevsky's *The Double* the central character's projected duplication of himself is experienced as a persecutory delusion consistent with the paranoid nature of his personality.

Rank's major psychological interest is what the frequent appearance of the double motif in literature may reveal of the character of the authors who are attracted to this theme. In his search for "the identical psychic structure of these authors" he finds them all "decidedly pathological personalities" who, in more than one direction, went beyond even that limit of neurotic conduct otherwise allowed to the artist."[3] E. T. A. Hoffman suffered from hallucinations in which he often saw before him his living mirror-image; the same is true of Jean Paul of whom it is said that in early childhood he had the sudden insight that "I am an I." This precocious self-awareness continued throughout his life as an uncanny projection of himself and found expression in his stories in the artistic reproduction of his delusional fantasies. The tragedy of Poe's life is well-known, filled as it was with habitual drinking and the excessive use of opium. His story of William Wilson is regarded as a personal confession. The autobiographical nature of the double, often presented in a most pathological form in the works of Friedrich Raimund and Dostoyevsky, are only too apparent. In fact, a biographer of Dostoyevsky, Dmitry Merezhkovsky describes his morbidity as poking around "in the most terrible and disgraceful abscesses of the human soul. . . . all the tragic, struggling couples among his most vividly real characters . . . turn out to be actually only the two halves of a third, cloven entity, who mutually seek and pursue each other as doubles."[4] The "cloven entity" would seem to be Dostoyevsky himself, whose fragmented self is projected onto the pages of his tragic writings.

It is no secret that there are clearly autobiographical elements in the works of all creative individuals—a fact known only too well to Rank whose special interest from an early age was the artist. But the motif of the double as it is expressed in literature seems to point to especially severe pathology on the part of those authors who portray this theme. Rank sums up the psychological commonality among the literary figures he has discussed:[5]

> The pathological disposition toward psychological disturbances is conditioned to a large degree by the splitting of the personality, with special emphasis upon the ego-complex, to which corresponds an abnormally strong interest in one's own person, his psychic states, and his destinies. This point of view leads to the characteristic relationship . . . to the world, to life, and particularly to the love-object, to which no harmonious relationship is found. Either the direct inability to love or . . . an exorbitantly strained longing for love characterize the two poles of this over-exaggerated attitude toward one's own ego. The various forms taken by the theme we have been treating are similar even down to slight details.

Thus Rank found in literature examples of narcissistic personality disorder which much later were to be explored clinically by such investigators as Kohut and Kernberg.

However, despite his awareness of the pathology in the creative personalities who produced the works of literature in which the theme of the double is central, Rank was not satisfied that this motif was merely an expression of psychopathology, nor did he think it could be explained solely in terms of the individual psychology of the personalities involved. He sensed in it a universality, an applicability to all human experience: "In the writer, as in the reader, a superindividual factor seems to be unconsciously vibrating here, lending to these motifs a mysterious psychic resonance."[6]

Rank turns to anthropology in an attempt to understand the universality of the theme of the double through its reflection in folklore, legend, and mythology. The superstitions abounding among primitive peoples, as reported in the works of Frazer, Negelein, Rohde, and others, that concern some aspect of the double center primarily around the relationship to the shadow and to the mirror-image. The shadow as a duplication of the self is surrounded by innumerable fears, superstitions, and taboos; many have to do with death, with health, with fertility. The failure to cast a shadow is frequently associated with death. The size of one's shadow is an indicator of health or illness, strength or weakness. In certain primitive cultures a belief exists that a woman can be impregnated by a shadow. The shadow is the soul, the guardian spirit, or a pursuing and torturing conscience. The mirror-image or reflection is surrounded by similar superstitions and taboos. Often they involve the fear of death or, as in the legend of Narcissus, they combine "the ruinous and the erotic";[7] for it was through the love of his own reflection that Narcissus ultimately met his end.

The love of self, for which we use the term narcissism as derived from the Greek legend, is paradoxical. It serves the self-preservative instinct and fosters the emergence and development of a unique individuality. Yet through the very fact of an awareness of this self it introduces the possibility of a limitation in the capacity for relatedness to others, and generates a fear of the loss of this precious self through death. These universal byproducts of human consciousness are responsible for the defensive operations which are manifested in the projection of a "double"—a replication of some part of the self which the individual can love or reject or feel comforted by the belief in its perpetuity. It is the immortal soul.

"The various taboos, precautions and evasions which primitive man uses with regard to his shadow show equally well his narcissistic esteem of his ego and his tremendous fear of it being threatened. Primitive narcissism feels itself primarily threatened by the ineluctable destruction of the self. Very clear evidence of the truth of this observation is shown by the choice, as the most primitive concept of the soul, of an image as closely similar as possible to the physical self, hence a true double. The idea of death, therefore, is denied by a duplication of the self incorporated in the shadow or in the reflected image."[8]

It is in his last work concerning the double that Rank transcends his own earlier understanding of the phenomenology of this motif as it is reflected in literature and mythology, and links the belief in an *immortal soul* to the need for an *immortal self*.[9] For it is not only in the primitive conceptions of the shadow or of the reflected image that death is denied. The perpetuity of the self is safeguarded in the very creation of culture itself.

Rank's understanding the development of culture, or of civilization as it relates to the need for immortality, is unique and its relationship to the theme of the double quite subtle. He begins by differentiating the *super* natural from the natural world. The supernatural is the *human* element which represents a need for spiritual values. It is beyond nature not in the sense of being divine or opposed to what is human, but as that spiritual aspect of the human outside the purely biological and material. In this sense the biological inevitably implies death, whereas a supernatural worldview offers limitless opportunity for the elaboration of the spiritual through the creation of what is outside nature—the concrete symbols which meet man's need for immortality. These symbols are represented in religion, art, literature, philosophy, psychology, and in social institutions: in all that we call culture. And it is through either a concrete contribution to culture or an identification with certain elements within it that the individual self finds immortality. Thus the culture of primitive man has this in common with our own: through its creation and existence in response to an inner spiritual need it assures the eternal survival of the self.

How is the theme of the double related to the need for immortalization of the self as it is expressed in culture? In primitive cultures the duality of the natural and the spiritual self were dynamically balanced through a magic worldview. In modern culture the harmonious integration of this duality has given way, because of what Rank calls the "overcivilized ego" (with its overemphasized rational worldview) to another conflictful duality: to a splitting of the self into two opposing selves, that of the acting self and that of the thinking and feeling self. The axis of this split is not the same as that between the dualism of the natural and the spiritual self; it is the conflict between "doing" and "feeling." The integration of this dichotomy within the self depends on whether the evaluation of the double as the immortal soul is positive or negative in the worldview of modern man. In other words, the spiritual self (the double) which creates culture is in turn evaluated by it and the nature of this evaluation determines the extent to which it becomes an integral part of the self. A positive evaluation creates the building up of the prototype of personality from the self; a negative evaluation—a conception of the double as the symbol of death—results in disintegration and is symptomatic of the conflict of many modern personality types. By analogy one is led to see in Rank's understanding of the integration of the self, as it reflects a cultural attitude toward its spiritual needs, a parallel with Kohut's conception of the development of the individual self. Its cohesion reflects the nature of the mother's feelings about her child in what she mirrors to him or her, be it affirmative, ambivalent, negative or insufficient.

In discussing the relationship of culture to the theme of the Double, Rank refers to the frequent appearance of the cult of twins as one of the earliest personifications of the double. Anthropology, history, folklore and literature are replete with the legendry, the taboos, the superstitions, and the humor that surround the phenomenon of twinship. He writes: "I believe that the heroic type emerged from the cult of twins and the self-creative tendency symbolized in the magic meaning of twinship. As the twins appear to have created themselves independently of natural procreation, so they were believed to be able to create things which formerly did not exist in nature—that is, what is called culture. This idea of the self-creative principle symbolized in twin-ship leads to the conception of the hero as the type who combines in one person the mortal and immortal self."[10]

The hero in turn is the cultural ego-ideal, the maker of history, the leader, the savior, the inspiration for the artist and writer. "The Greek artist took all his inspirations from commonly known episodes in the lives of the nation's heroes, thereby expressing artistically his own creative self shaped after the heroic type of action. In this sense, the true artist type may be thought of as the hero's spiritual double, who told in immortal works of art what the other had done and thus preserved the memory of it and himself for posterity." Thus the motif of the double achieves creative significance. It permeates the mythology of many peoples. In Hindu cosmogony in more abstract form the *reflection* of the first Being was the cause of the material world. In the Book of Genesis, God created man in his own image. In one version of the Greek myth, Dionysus "was said to have been conceived by his mother Persephone as she admired herself in a mirror," and he in turn, as he gazed at himself in a mirror, was "seduced by the reflection and created the external world in his own image."[11]

Some years ago a female patient reported a dream to me in which the mirror-image is clearly connected with creation. She was a young married woman, at the time pregnant with her first child. In her own childhood she had had a very symbiotic relationship with her mother. There were still residues of this emotional overdependency at the time of the

dream. It was a simple dream but one frought with mixed emotions of
fear, almost horror, yet fascination. She dreamed that *she looked into a
mirror and beheld her mother's face* instead of her own. In the formation of
her personality, her own double (and actually there was great physical
resemblance between herself and her mother) was the mother with whose
introjected image she was still merged. In anticipation of motherhood
she had to create herself as a mother through an identification with her
own mother, which she expressed concretely in the dream through the
mirror image.

But the emotions of fear and dread which accompany this projection
speak for the fact that her own creation of a child heralds a separation
from her symbiotic mother relationship in which she is the child and
announces her emergence as a discrete person and mother. The dream
is a dream of a double not in the simple sense of a likeness, or a reflection.
Instead, the dream reveals the workings of an inner conflictful psychological process in which the identification with the role (mother) must
be partially detached from a merging identification with the particular
individual mother in the name of separation and the achievement of one's
unique identity. The double is thus not a mere recapitulation of the past,
but a creative announcement of the prospective emergence of the self.
The prospective aspect of duplication precipitates yet a further conflict
around the theme of the double which is expressed in the conflict of
generations. For the older generation, immortality is achieved through
a certain duplication and perpetuation in the succeeding generation. Yet,
if the child resembles the parent too closely both fear a loss of individuality. Among some primitive peoples, Rank notes, there exists the belief
"apparent in the father's fear that if the child bears too great resemblance
to him he is doomed to die; the idea being that it has taken from him
his image or shadow, that is to say, his soul."[12] For the child, too, the
extreme likeness may be experienced as a threat to his individuality. Yet
it may also be helpful, provided the identification is a predominantly
positive one in the structuring of the self.

In discussing the narcissistic personality as the dominant type in contemporary society, Christopher Lasch notes that for individuals within
a society governed by the cult of youth, old age is experienced with
dread because of a loss of faith in the future, in the regeneration of life.

Among "the traditional consolations of old age, the most important
. . . is the belief that future generations will in some sense carry [one's]
life's work. Love and work unite in a concern for posterity, and specifically in an attempt to equip the younger generation to carry on the tasks
of the older. The thought that we live on vicariously in our children
(more broadly, in future generations) reconciles us to our own super-
session. . . . When the generational link begins to fray, such consolations
no longer obtain."[13]

Thus in cultural evolution there is an oscillation between a tradition-
alism in which perpetuity through succeeding generations is assured, and
an assertion of individualism, often accompanied by an exaggerated importance of self, which threatens a sense of immortality. Rank perceived
this conflict and saw it reflected in the theme of the double.

The understanding of the self-creative principle which informs Rank's
work throughout as well as its relationship to culture characterizes his
explanation of the theme of the double and carries it beyond an interpretation of narcissistic phenomena, either as a phase of individual development or as pathology, to an explanation of a crucial factor in the
evolution of culture. If one were to summarize in schematic form the
meaning of the double in Rank's thinking, it would run something like
this: Man has a fundamental need to immortalize his hard-won self—his
double, either as shadow, mirror-image, conscience or alter-ego as these
roles are depicted in mythology, superstition, and literature. This need
serves the function of self-perpetuation. However, on the primitive narcissistic level of self-duplication, the double does not serve the creation
of cultures. It is later in human history, Rank believes, that the hero and
the artist renounce

"the egotistic principle of self-perpetuation in one's own image" and substitute for it "the perpetuation of the self in work reflecting one's personality. . . . This idea of a self-creative power attributed to certain individuals
signified a decisive step beyond the naïve belief in an automatic survival of
one's own double, in that it impressed upon man the conviction that he has
to work for his immortality by creating lasting achievements. In this sense,
the great Alberti, in the early fifteenth century, could say that when Narcissus saw his reflection in the water and trembled at the beauty of his own
face he was the real inventor of painting.[14]

It is through this perception of the creative aspect of self-love as it is manifested in the striving toward individuation and projected in cultural achievements that Rank carries the motif of the double into the mainstream of his theories, thus transcending the more primitive view of the Double as a way to immortality through simple narcissistic self-perpetuation in one's own image.

TEN

_____

Psychotherapy

ALTHOUGH THE *Trauma of Birth*, which initiated the split between Freud and Rank, was published in 1923, it was not until 1931 that Rank ceased to think of himself as a psychoanalyst. In the intervening years he wrote extensively on his philosophy of therapy, on his conception of therapeutic procedure, on a theory of personality, and on the human situation. He completed two prodigious works: one, the *Technique of Psychoanalysis* in three volumes and the other, *Outlines of a Genetic Psychology on the Basis of the Psychoanalysis of the Ego Structure*, also in three volumes. In both works he used the terminology of psychoanalysis, retaining the term psychoanalysis in the titles, as Jessie Taft tells us, because of an agreement with his publisher.[1] However, as he approached the third volume of these works, his deviation from the orthodox Freudian point of view both in theory and practice became clear to him. But it was not until the English translation of *parts* of these works (vols. 2 and 3 of *Technique*, and vol. 3 of *Genetic Psychology*) was undertaken that he realized the central role of the creative will in his thinking about the development of personality and its treatment, and agreed to call his analytic work, both theoretical and practical, *Will Therapy*.

This gradual evolution beyond Freudian psychoanalysis not only in regard to the products of Rank's thinking, but in his very self-conception illustrates the essence of his view of human development and informs his philosophy of treatment. It is a view in which the goal is constructive rather than analytic, and which therefore addresses itself primarily to a growth process rather than to an interpretation of content. If it can be said of Freud that he discovered psychoanalysis and the dynamic unconscious through the understanding and interpretation of symbolic processes in dreams—largely his own—it can be said of Rank that he achieved a profound understanding of the development and creation of the self through his own growth.

In Rank's philosophy of therapy we find the summation of his theory of creativity and of his psychology of the will. In his phrase "the volitional affirmation of the obligatory" (see chapter 3), he expressed not only his philosophy of life, but his goal for psychotherapy as well. Therapy should be geared to the cultivation of the creative will; in this sense it is volitional, striving to liberate the individual's inherent capacities. It should help the individual to accept the nature of his own being and of his emotional life; in this sense it is affirmative. It should foster an awareness of the duality of life and death, thus placing the obligatory and the inevitable in perspective.

Clearly this existential approach to therapy is not without explicit and implicit values. It values the individual in his uniqueness and his capacity for understanding and feeling, growth, and creativity. Unlike classic psychoanalysis, which claims to operate outside the realm of values (unless it be that of understanding), Rank argues that by its very nature psychotherapy is morally or at least normatively oriented.[2] "Whether it has to do with the medical concept of normality or with the social concept of adaptation, therapy can never be without prejudice for it sets out from the standpoint that something should be otherwise than it is, no matter how one may formulate it."[3] Psychology, on the other hand, attempts to describe what is and, where possible, why it is so. It must stand, therefore, in inherent opposition to therapy which is corrective from the standpoint of a particular set of values.

Psychoanalysis began as therapy, and the knowledge it derived from that procedure is therefore inevitably colored by the norms it held— norms which in turn reflected the social mores and conventions of the time in which it originated as well as the values and idiosyncrasies of particular individual therapists. Because of the contradiction which resides in the *aims* of psychotherapy and psychology, and the confusion which psychoanalysis has created by denying this incongruity, Rank opposes Freud's formation of universal psychological theories especially as applied in therapy, since they disregard the social framework, the uniqueness of each individual, and the psychology of the therapist. He regards the need for the certainty of a theory as a longing to hold on to something constant, and since the psychic is in constant change and movement, a psychological theory must inevitably destroy some aspect of psychic reality, especially if its function is to support a particular therapeutic approach.

Psychic reality in Rank's view is grasped not so much through interpretive knowledge as through experience. Therefore, therapy is less a process of acquiring understanding than of experiencing one's own functioning in the context of a new relationship.

To be therapeutic the experience must affirm the individual's will and help him or her to accept it rather than to condemn it. It is an exercise in the justification of the will as it expresses the uniqueness and autonomy of the self. In contrast, psychoanalysis, by describing the *impulses* as unconscious and universal, has given the individual a justification for them by declaring them universal, thus absolving the individual from responsibility for them. Nevertheless, Rank concludes, there is a limited and temporary therapeutic value even in such reassurance from an authority figure (doctor or priest) that the impulses are not evil, especially for individuals "who always seek some kind of excuse for their willing and find it now in the id instead of in God."[4]

"The wish for permission to will autonomously is a measure of the guilt associated with such an act." This was brought home to me most dramatically when a patient turned to me toward the end of her treatment and with much emotion expressed the wish that I say to her, *"Timschel"* (Hebrew for "Thou mayest").[5] It was only when she felt my acceptance of her individuality that she could accept her own willing with a manageable quantity of guilt, and could accept others in their unique autonomy. The result was a striking improvement in her interpersonal relationships as well as in her own contentment.

Each individual is unique and the therapist, sensing the essence of the patient's individuality, must interact with this uniqueness. In fact it is the therapist's very perception of this distinctiveness that marks the beginning of his affirmation of the patient's individuality, thus enabling the patient to accept himself and his own will—the will which is the *individuated* function of the ego—through identification with the therapist.

It is not surprising that, given Rank's philosophical approach to human life and to the therapeutic process, he would not view neurosis from the perspective of psychoanalysis. Certainly for him neurosis is not a medical problem nor primarily a sexual one, but a profoundly human one, a disturbance in ego functioning. Emotional suffering is inevitable, and the neurosis is a disturbance in the ability to adapt felicitously to this inevitability. But while it is a maladaptation, Rank sees it nevertheless as a creative endeavor to adapt and to achieve expressiveness. He regards the neurotic as a creative type who has failed and refers to him as an *artiste manqué*. Since so many artist types combine neurotic with artistic elements, Rank compares the two, seeing the true artist as one who uses his creativity to objectify the emotional suffering in his work, not as a direct projection of self, but as a creative reworking of his emotions through the art form. The neurotic, on the other hand, is inhibited from positively expressing his creative will. He is immured in his introspective concern with self, thus giving up true spontaneity.

The therapeutic importance of a view of neurosis as a creative process, however unsuccessful, lies in the absence of condemnation, in its respect for individual effort, and therefore by implication in the hope for further growth. In the acceptance of emotional suffering as an existential fact of life, the illusion that it can be avoided through proper upbringing is disspelled and the individual is called upon to assume responsibility for his own adaptation to the painfulness of certain aspects of life. Rank would certainly not deny the value of an optimally loving environment for the healthy development of the child's growing self; but he was sensitive to the fallacy implied in the strictly deterministic view of classic psychoanalysis, which, by placing the causality for the dynamics of neurosis in the historical development of the instinct life as it unfolded in the family setting, neglected the dimension of ego growth and thus tended to absolve the individual from responsibility for his own unique adaptation. The "blame" for neurosis fell too exclusively on parents, who bore an excessive burden of guilt: they felt that had they "done everything right" the child would not be maladjusted. As we have already seen in chapter 5, guilt is not primarily the result of unacceptable impulses; it is an ego phenomenon—the inevitable byproduct of individuation and of creative activity, especially as it is expressed in "willing." The suffering associated with it, as well as the responsibility for mastering it, must be borne by each individual.

Rank's therapeutic procedures were modified in the course of his development, as were his psychological and philosophical views of man. However, his concern with and understanding of the creative process of individuation remained constant. In the early phases of his work, it appears when the issue of separation from the mother was paramount in his mind (see chapter 6) and he perceived the analytic task as one in which the trauma of the first separation had to be overcome by reenacting the birth experience in the treatment. The nature of the analytic situation—the authority of the therapist, the prone position of the patient, the darkened room, and the instruction to the patient to express whatever occurred in his mind—contributed to the promotion of regression. It was through this regressive process, aided by the setting of a terminal date, that Rank hoped to help the patient, through emotional discharge, to effect and complete a separation from the mother which was not sufficiently abreacted during the actual birth experience. Here we see Rank thinking in the Freudian terms of discharge of pent-up energy and its resolution in the transference relationship to the therapist. But even at this level of Rank's development there is an important difference: they both consider regression to be essential to the treatment, but Freud sees this repetition in the transference as serving the ultimate renunciation of instinctual gratification, while Rank sees the actuality of the analytic situation as serving separation—i.e., the ultimate development of autonomy on the part of the patient. For Rank, then, therapy is a process of ego growth.

In discussing *The Trauma of Birth* at the time of its fiftieth anniversary, Ekstein says of Rank's therapeutic approach: it "leads to a positive concept of psychotherapy in which he [Rank] stresses the processes of development, and thus he becomes indirectly an initiator of new thinking which sees the educator not simply as a preventer of emotional illness but as someone who creates opportunities for growth, for unfolding, birth-giving."[6]

The primary obstacle to growth—to the inhibition of the ability to will and to express emotion spontaneously—is the unresolved symbiotic relationship to the mother, and the wish to stay merged with her. Rank hoped to create the opportunity for growth by so structuring the analytic situation as to induce the anxiety experienced at birth by setting a time limit for the treatment. In this maneuver Rank addressed himself to what he saw as the crucial issue: the patient's fixation on the bond with the mother and his or her inability to sever this connection. The issue of separation was thus forced into the central focus of treatment. By emphasizing the separation from the analyst from the beginning of the analysis, separation could be accomplished gradually and in the final phase of treatment the patient would not be overwhelmed by an unconscious reproduction of the birth trauma and could thus deal more fully with his or her current conflicts.[7]

In *Technik der Psychoanalyse*, Rank's directives and criteria for the setting of a terminal date are quite structured and specific. He says that the analyst must make the estimate as soon as possible, on the basis of the unconscious derivatives which the patient expresses when he begins to relate to the analyst in the same infantile manner as he did to his mother. When this crucial point is reached, the analyst must make certain that what was formerly a mother fixation does not become a fixation on the analyst. The analyst achieves this by making the patient conscious of the pattern, as well as by his own behavior. Rank points out that the terminal date will vary in individual cases. In this connection he distinguishes two distinct types of patient. Those types who develop a positive transference very rapidly will experience a longer and more difficult ending phase. On the other hand, narcissistic types often begin with a negative transference and a skeptical attitude; it will take a longer time for them to develop a positive transference. In their cases, however, the ending phase of treatment (relative to the development of a good relationship with the analyst) will be short.[8]

Ekstein, reporting a personal communication with Virginia Robinson who experienced analysis with Otto Rank, says that as far as she knew in the late twenties and early thirties Rank was not using a *fixed time limit* [italics mine] for beginning and ending but "made use of ending with each patient differently."[9] This is consistent with Rank's respect for the uniqueness of each individual and his increasing emphasis on the function of "willing" as the expression of this uniqueness.

As Rank moved away from a literal conception of therapy as psychologically reproducing the biological experience of birth, he focused on individuation as the process through which the ego is structured as it emerges from its embeddedness in the mother relationship. The neurotic individual, who has achieved individuation too exclusively through negative will, is caught in a conflict between the expression of his autonomy, which depends on opposition and the wish to love significant others in his life. His "negative willing" has interfered with his "loving"; the striving for separateness has precluded the possibility of a loving relationship to the "thou" in the world and has thus, to some extent, distorted the individual's perception of the real world.

Therapy must therefore restore to the neurotic individual the possibility of willing and loving in a balanced way—that is, of creating a loving relationship within the context of his own individuated self. This can be accomplished through the analyst's *acceptance* of the patient, which is the primary curative factor.[10] To understand what Rank means by acceptance we must concern ourselves with his distinctive conception of the place of the emotions in human life. After discussing the ego's development from the object relationship in the first volume of *Genetic Psychology*, Rank asks the question: What force "keeps all these processes going and gives the impulse power to all these mechanisms?" That force is the emotions.[11] Ego psychology deals with the study of mechanisms, whereas a "thou psychology" deals with relationship to others and is, according to Rank, the central and real sphere of psychology. Here Rank foreshadows the modern object-relations theorists—Fairbairn, Guntrip, Winicott.

It is the love feeling, originating in the child's feeling toward the mother,

which unites our ego with the other, with the Thou, with the world and so does away with all fear. But what is unique in love is that beyond the fact of uniting, it rebounds on the ego. Not only, I love the other as my ego, as part of my ego, but the other also makes my ego worthy of love. The love of the Thou thus places a value on one's own ego. Love abolishes egoism, it merges the self in the other to find it again enriched in one's own ego. This unique projection and introjection of feeling rests on the fact that one can really only love the one who *accepts* our own self as it is, indeed will not have it otherwise than it is, and whose self we accept as it is.[12]

The love-feeling is based on identification; it creates the ability to identify.

Speaking of the therapeutic situation, Rank emphasizes that it is a learning process not in the intellectual sense, but in the emotional sense. In the course of it the therapist's acceptance, precisely in terms of the identification just mentioned, is crucial: the patient learns to recognize his "true self" in the mirror of the other.[13] This is reminiscent of the current work of Kohut, in which he attributes the origins of the child's self feeling to the mother's mirroring back to him her feelings about him. He sees himself in her eyes, and derives his self-image from her.

Should the love feeling not be reciprocated, the identity—in the sense of oneness and likeness—with the loved one is destroyed and a painful feeling of isolation and separation results. To master this painful feeling the ego of the individual denies the absence of love in the world of reality and creates, in his inner world of the emotions, an illusion of oneness with the love object. As Kohut puts it: "The feeling says: this identity between me and the other exists because it exists in me."[14] This is a denial of difference and of separation. For Rank "denial" refers, therefore, not to a direct falsification of an unpleasant external reality or of an unacceptable impulse, but to the *creation*, through processes of projection and introjection, of an *inner illusion, whose function it is to obscure the reality of separation from a love object.* Should denial alone be an insufficient defense, the ego then attempts to eliminate the source of pain by absorbing it into itself.[15] Denial, the creation of illusory emotion, and identification are thus defensive operations instituted to master the fear of separation—a fear which makes its first appearance early in the mother–child relationship.

Before discussing the import of these mechanisms for psychotherapy, it might be well to ask why the fear of separation, the fear of becoming autonomous, is so overriding in human life. Not, as Rank thought originally, because the biological birth process was so traumatic for the human infant in terms of being overwhelmed by unassimilable stimuli that it became the psychological paradigm for all future anxieties. Nor, as Freud and M. Klein would have it, because in the condition of extreme helplessness and dependence that is the child's lot during a prolonged period of development, he must find psychological ways of dealing with the inevitable pain resulting from the frustration of instinct needs—especially on the oral level. The pain is then translated into fear of separation, since the mother is the source of instinctual gratification.

There is some truth in both views, yet in relation to separation both miss the implication that in the human condition of extreme helplessness there must be a dim, instinctive awareness that there is dependence for the development of the very instrument of autonomy—the ego—on the *psychological nourishment* which derives from the mother. Simply stated, one needs mother love for the ego growth through which one then becomes separate and individuated. The child, sensing his or her incompleteness, fears separation because he or she lacks the resources to deal independently with the world of reality as well as with his or her own inner world. To some extent it is a fear which persists throughout life, since no one achieves complete independence in all life situations. Yet when it exists in extreme form it is the hallmark of a failure in development, a faulting in the ego, and of a neurotic disturbance which interferes with an individual's functioning. For this reason, as Rank so rightly perceived, the issue of psychological separation stands in the center of the therapeutic process.

In the course of clinical work, the patient's fear of separation from the therapist often manifests itself dramatically as a period of vacation approaches. Such an incident occurred in my own practice.[16]

Ruth, as I shall call her, is a young woman who came to treatment because her relationships with people, especially men, were unsatisfactory and because she was having great difficulty completing her dissertation for a doctorate in psychology. It is important to know that on the day on which the explosive event, which I am about to describe, occurred she had just turned in the first draft of her dissertation.

It was the next to the last session before vacation. She stormed into my office in a rage because I had kept her waiting for a few minutes. This was not the first time that she had been angered by having to wait but, although she was aware that I have often generously given her more than her allotted time, this fact did not dispel her paranoid-compulsive feeling that I do this intentionally to demean her. She experienced having to wait as a sign of my disrespect and lack of consideration. Finally, she confessed that she had long thought of leaving her therapy because of this. I pointed out the displacement of her rage at being abandoned (the vacation) onto the issue of time, and made clear that whenever she interprets an event as abandonment, she leaves first, before she can be left. This has been a pattern in her life. When things don't go her way, she leaves—her friends, her boyfriend, her colleagues. In this instance, my casualness about time was not to her liking. She abusively demanded that I change, or she threatened to leave.

What begins to emerge is the struggle of wills. The therapeutic situation, which by its very nature I am empowered to set up (e.g., the time of vacation, the time for the beginning of her session), is one to which she is afraid to yield because it connotes both separation and merging. She fights for her autonomy with counter-will. Her words were: "I am at your mercy." My answer was that, while I possibly was too casual about time, I certainly had no intention of demeaning her, and that she would have to take me as I am if she wanted to continue working with me. But I said more: I remarked that my time was valuable, that I had counted on her continuing treatment in the fall, had reserved time for her, and that it was unfair of her to let me know at this late date that she did not wish to continue. I do not usually speak this way to a patient. I do not usually invoke the value of my time to create separation between us, and I might not have done so on this occasion if I had not a few hours before found it necessary to turn someone away who was eager to come into treatment with me, for lack of time. But what I had done without forethought, as a result of my spontaneous emotion of annoyance and anger, had an electrifying effect on my patient, which became manifest in the following and final session of the season, which occurred two days later.

My patient came in, in a much calmer state, saying: "It clicked, when I thought it over; the key word was 'unfair.' I realize that the unfair thing was that I felt no gratitude for all your help with the dissertation." I had not had this particular meaning of "unfair" in mind; but I let it stand, because intuitively I realized that she was struggling to give up an old pattern, to effect change in her own attitudes, and to use the conflict between us creatively.

What had happened, to my mind, was that in Ruth's case, the word "unfair" had put the distance essential for individuation between us. She was able to perceive me, my needs, my reactions as separate and different from hers, and to realize the inappropriateness of her emotion relative to my having helped her to succeed in the very thing for which she had come for help—the finishing of the dissertation. But it was precisely this accomplishment, as well as my leaving on vacation, which precipitated the fear that in turn produced the angry chaotic and neurotic reactions of the previous session. For the dissertation in its symbolic meaning is an "end," a statement of self. It represents a leaving of dependency and of childhood. As Ruth spoke of these feelings she suddenly recalled that June had always been for her a month of depression and anxiety. Throughout her childhood it had meant separation—especially separation from school, which she loved and which was a refuge for her from a stormy familial environment. Suddenly it occurred to her that June was the time of her younger brother's birth, when her mother had left her to go to the hospital for the delivery, had become seriously ill after the baby's birth, and had remained in the hospital for three months. Ruth, who was three years old at the time, was cared for by a neighbor into whose large family of children she was absorbed. When her mother returned she resisted returning to her parents' home. Out of the feeling of having been abandoned, she rejected her mother emotionally, yet subsequently sought the ancient symbiosis in every relationship. My upcoming vacation, the all-but-completed dissertation, and her brother's birthday converged to press upon her the unconscious memory of an unresolved separation conflict. Up to this point in her life, she had attempted to resolve it by a revengeful, angry act of "leaving"—an act in which, because she actively took the initiative, gave her the illusion of functioning independently. She took the act of counter-will as one of positive willing.

In the two sessions I have described she relived with great affect the inappropriate displacement onto the therapist of the rage which she felt as a small child when her mother left her—physically, to give birth to her brother, and emotionally, through her concerns for another child (the phenomenon referred to in Freudian analysis as transference); and she arrived at an understanding of the meaning and implication of those memories and their connections with her current life. However, I doubt that all this in itself would have had sufficient therapeutic impact to effect a change in her. The "therapeutic moment" came when, in the stark realization of our distinct and separate individualities, she responded to the possibility within her own personality of a new, a changed reaction. She took the responsibility for a "volitional affirmation of the obligatory," in which the "obligatory" is the inevitable fact of our difference, and the "volitional affirmation" is a positive, rather than negative and reactive, act of creative will which uses the "inevitable" to promote growth and maturation, in fact, to structure an increasingly individuated self.

The felicitous outcome of these sessions does not, however, answer the question of what enabled Ruth to use the experience creatively; it does not necessarily follow that the patient will be able to make this choice even if the therapist, inspired by Rank, is oriented to the mobilization of the patient's responsibility for the creative development of his or her own autonomy. The ability to choose growth and change creatively rather than to persist in the repetition of neurotic patterns depends on so many factors as well as on their complex interactions, that we can never know with certainty which elements are crucial. First, there is the enormous variability in the initial constitutional endowment of individuals. Ruth, for example, had tremendous vitality and energy from the first, and was readily able to find satisfaction—sometimes with a slight touch of grandiosity—in her own competent functioning in the external world. Her defensive reactions to anxiety were largely, though not entirely, projections of blame upon other individuals.

Yet, despite inherent differences among individuals and despite widely divergent life experiences, with consequent variations in ways of adapting, the ability of a particular patient to choose growth—i.e., to affirm the direction of the life stream, and to take responsibility for change and the fulfillment of his or her own capacities—will depend greatly on the therapist's belief in the human capacity to creatively structure and restructure personality, and on his or her ability to convey this to the patient. Just as a child's growth is enhanced by the mother's belief in and affirmation of it, so for the patient who has generally lacked such affirmation in childhood, the experience of the therapist's belief in and respect for his or her separate and distinct individuality creates the atmosphere of trust in which the patient can dare to will change. It is initially to Rank that we owe this insight into the development and function of the will, and its creative use in the structuring of personality.

Once an individual has been freed of the compulsion to repeat the past through insight, the opportunity exists in the actuality of the relationship to the therapist in the therapeutic situation to exercise his or her will for change. This spontaneous, individual act of will then bridges a gap between the present and the future, thus instituting a new chain of causality—a specifically human, psychological causality which differs from the historically rooted causality of the natural sciences. (Even in the natural sciences determinism is by no means absolute.) The causality created by the exercise of will corresponds to the randomness of nature, since it is unpredictable in each individual instance. Willing is an expression of the creation of something new, of a freeing of oneself from the exclusive influence of the past. Man is the beginning of a new series of causes and his mythological heroes, through their will to be free of the past, symbolize the creative nature of this will: the biblical Adam through the beginning of a new species; Prometheus through the creation of a new generation; Christ through the inauguration of a new age. In this view of human psychology we see clearly its derivation from Rank's concern with the creative individual.

Nowhere is Rank's insistence on the important meaning of the analytic situation for the implementation of will more clearly exemplified than in his analysis of the famous dream from Freud's well-known case of the Wolfman, entitled in Freud's writings: "From the History of an Infantile Neurosis." His understanding of the dream differs radically from Freud's historical-causal interpretation. Rank would refer to his own interpretation as genetic-constructive. Rank's use of the dream is so illustrative of his therapeutic approach that it is worth narrating the dream and Rank's interpretation.[17]

The Wolfman, so named because of his dream, a severely disturbed young man, whom today we would call borderline, was a Russian who came to Freud when he was about 25. He was the only son of an extremely wealthy family with an aristocratic lifestyle. The family was burdened with mental and emotional ills. The father was severely depressed, the mother was not only physically ailing, but also hypochondriacal. The patient's sister (his only sibling) tended to be sadistic toward her younger brother, became emotionally disturbed in adolescence, and committed suicide in her early twenties. He grew up on a large estate in an atmosphere of loneliness, and of essential emotional abandonment by his parents, who often went off on trips leaving him in charge of a governess of the children. From early childhood he was cared for by his beloved Nanya (nursemaid) whom he loved more than his parents. He was a fearful child and his sister further aroused his anxieties by teasing him to the point of precipitating a temper tantrum.

Surrounded by superstition, by stories of atrocities and of sadistic punishments, he clung to his Nanya; his early years were dominated by severe neurotic disturbances even before the appearance of an animal phobia in his fourth year. The phobia was inaugurated by the famous Wolfman dream on his fourth birthday, which fell on Christmas Eve. The dream runs as follows:

> I dreamt that it was night and that I was lying in my bed. (My bed stood with its foot towards the window; in front of the window there was a row of old walnut trees. I know it was winter when I had the dream, and night-time.) Suddenly the window opened of its own accord, and I was terrified to see that some white wolves were sitting on the big walnut tree in front of the window. There were six or seven of them. The wolves were quite white, and looked more like foxes or sheep-dogs, for they had big tails like foxes and they had their ears pricked like dogs when they pay attention to something. In great terror, evidently of being eaten up by the wolves, I screamed and woke up. My nurse hurried to my bed, to see what had happened to me.

The dream was a nightmare of early childhood and was told and retold a number of times during the Wolfman's analysis with Freud. Freud finally set a terminal date for the analysis, because the patient was "un-assailably entrenched behind an attitude of obliging apathy,"

> under the inexorable pressure of this fixed limit his resistance and his fixation to the illness gave way, and now in a disproportionately short time the analysis produced all the material which made it possible to clear up his inhibitions and remove his symptoms. All the information, too, which enabled me to understand his infantile neurosis is derived from this last period of the work.[18]

It is ironic that Freud used a technique—the setting of a terminal date—in the name of uncovering the past and producing derivatives of the unconscious, which Rank later used with an entirely different end in view: the patient's achieving separation and ego autonomy. Freud failed to realize that the production of all the material which enabled him to understand the Wolfman's infantile neurosis was a gift to Freud, an attempt to gain and hold his love, to avoid dealing with his ambivalence and to preserve the positive imago of the father figure. It therefore repeated and perpetuated the past for the patient. As his subsequent illness (treated by Ruth Mack Brunswick) and his later life show, he never became free of his neurotic attachment to Freud; he never achieved separateness and autonomy.[19]

By dealing with a long chain of the patient's associative thoughts, Freud arrived derivately at an interpretation of the dream which focuses on the assumption that there was an early sexual experience—the little boy's observation of the primal scene at the age of one and a half, which aroused confusion in sexual identity and castration anxiety. Freud considered the precipitating cause of the Wolfman's breakdown the fact that he acquired gonorrhea at the age of 18. This revived the threat of castration, threatened his masculine narcissism, and deprived him of a dearly held illusion that he was especially favored by destiny. Freud also regarded the patient as cured once all the *causal* connections between his early childhood impulses and experiences had been uncovered and understood in the light of the manner in which he had attempted to resolve them.

We know from the Wolfman's subsequent analysis with Ruth Mack Brunswick and his own account of his life, (in the course of which he was able to function in a limited and restricted way but never really achieved adult autonomy) that he was helped but certainly not cured. This does not necessarily reflect on the invalidity of Freudian libido theory, but it places in serious doubt the curative effect of a purely historical-causative approach to therapy.

I am reminded of a young woman patient who has been in a lengthy analysis for a severe sexual inhibition, and who recently reported a dream to me, the analysis of which revealed a rather obvious reference to incestuous impulses toward an older brother. Her associations led to recollections of sexual experiences in childhood with an uncle and a male cousin and seemed to confirm my impression of her feelings toward her brother. At this point she asked the question: "I wonder if I *really* had a sexual experience with my brother, or whether it was only a wish?"

I countered with the question: "And what difference would it make if something had really happened?"

"Well," she replied, "I feel that if I could uncover a real incident that is the *cause* of my difficulties, *somehow* this knowledge would make everything change."

In the word "somehow" is contained the magical expectation that betrays the passive stance of the patient's ego—the abnegation of responsibility for making use of her understanding, the denial of the function of her will.

It was to this issue of the role of will in the current life of my patient that Rank addressed himself in his theory of therapy. His interpretation of the Wolfman dream illustrates his emphasis on the patient's life of the present. In the first place, Rank views the dream as belonging to a category of typical dreams he had experienced in the analyses of a number of his patients: dreams which were precipitated by the analytic situation, especially by the setting of a terminal date; dreams which expressed the patient's wish to be included in the analyst's family or into the family of analysts. He calls these the dreams of the family tree, since the tree often appears in the dream as a symbol of the mother. The analytic situation harks back to its prototype, the mother situation, and the patient's wish is to return to the union with the mother, to cancel out the separation of birth. Although the dream of the Wolfman was dreamt on the eve of his fourth birthday—which seems to confirm its connection with birth and the mother—Rank feels justified in regarding it as a dream precipitated by the analytic situation, because it reappeared in the analysis in innumerable variations.

The analytic situation, because it invariably reconstitutes the family situation, stirs up old infantile jealousies; the element of sibling rivalry plays an important role in the dream of the Wolfman. The setting of the dream (the bed with its foot toward the window, the row of trees outside, the wolves sitting on the tree branches) duplicates the situation in Freud's office (the sofa facing the window, the chestnut trees which the patient could see looking out of the window, the pictures of Freud's disciples on the narrow wall beside the window, representing the siblings who form the family tree of psychoanalysis). The feeling of reality in the dream refers to the actuality of the current situation: the analysis with its inevitable separation from the analyst. In his associations to the fairy tales of his childhood, the Wolfman comforts himself in his birth fear by saying, as it were, "It is only a fairy tale." The feeling in the dream of being stared at by the wolves is the feeling of being observed by the analyst. But the patient himself is a voyeur; he wishes to see, not to be in the dark in the analysis: a reversal of the night time setting of the dream. In that "suddenly the window opens of itself" Rank sees a reference to birth (children are told that the stork brings babies through the window) and the wolves on the tree are his rivals—his sister and his father—who were on the family tree (on the mother) before him. The fear of being eaten by the wolves (of returning to the mother's stomach) is a turning of his own birth fear into the wish to send his sister back into the womb. Thus the Wolfman lives out in the analytic situation the infantile jealousy of his sister by transferring it to Freud's analytic family. The siblings are wished out of the way so that the mother can be possessed alone. And the analyst basically represents the mother.

One might object that Rank's interpretation of the dream symbolism is as much guesswork as is Freud's. And while this may be so, it would seem to me that the important factor is the therapeutic goal to which each person's interpretation is geared, regardless of the accuracy or inaccuracy of the content. Freud's goal was the discovery of causality in terms of how the early infantile, repressed impulses and experiences were responsible for the neurotic conflict. The uncovering of causality became curative. Rank's therapeutic goal, on the other hand, was concerned with individuation. By focusing on the mother relationship in the interaction with the therapist in emotional and experiential terms, Rank hoped to familiarize the patient with his paradoxical wishes for union with and separation from the mother and his fear of both, thus enabling him through self acceptance to become his own person.

Rank insisted on the analysis of the analytic situation, which he distinguished from the transference. This is a subtle distinction because on the face of it it would seem that what he is describing is in fact a mother transference. Yet this is not the case, for Rank does not regard the therapeutic relationship as merely a new edition of the past. The actual setting up of the analytic situation, the nature of the analyst's personality, and the emotional relationship of the patient to the analyst determine what will happen in the treatment as much as the patient's past childhood experiences. Through a consistent analysis of the actual analytic situation, the transference reactions are not cultivated as they are in a classic analysis, but are in effect pulled out by the roots—by the analysis of the mother bond. This is how one deals with the fear of living in the present, of being born as an autonomous self. Instead of the uncovering of the past, and the analysis of its influence on the present, the ego of the patient becomes the focus of the treatment, and his will to apply his knowledge and understanding, be it of the past or present, begins to be liberated.[20]

It is important to be clear that Rank at no point denies either the fact or the meaning of the historical past. However, he points out the difficulty of deciding how much of what appears as material in the analysis is truly historical, and what pathognomic importance is to be assigned to it. In the neglect of the analysis of the analytic situation, he sees the danger of projecting back into the past, and thus misusing it, events and reactions which really belong to the present.

Ferenczi took serious issue with Rank's approach in 1924.[21] He points out that while Rank rejects the historical point of view—and Rank does so only to the extent that he finds it therapeutically unproductive—he exaggerates a particular historic factor—birth—and hopes to resolve the trauma in the repetition of the birth-separation experience with the analyst. Ferenczi further criticizes Rank for placing the mother-bond rather than the castration complex at the core of the neurosis. It is true that Rank makes therapeutic use of a particular historic situation, in fact the earliest one in the life of an individual. But this situation and the historic past it represents belong to a different category than the past with which Freud is concerned. Freud was oriented to the libido theory; his concern with the past was with the uncovering of unconscious impulses, with the dynamics of their interaction with other parts of the personality, and with their ultimate fate in the formation of symptoms and of character. Rank's concern with the past has to do with the issue of separation of the individual as an autonomous entity from the matrix in which he was conceived and nurtured—in other words, with the issue of the development of individuation. This is ego psychology and one might say that Rank is the unacknowledged forerunner of the modern ego psychologists in the field of analysis. Almost before he was fully aware of it, and certainly before he was concerned with the problem of "will," he thought in ego-psychological rather than in predominently libido-theoretical terms; and with the growing awareness of how the use of the past might become therapeutically sterile, he felt the necessity for modifying his technique of treatment.

Possibly, understanding the past in terms of its unconscious dynamics could be useful for strengthening the ego. If so, it would not be because in itself the unconscious has been uncovered, but because the ego has the opportunity to perceive the total self, objectify it, and reintegrate it. However, the efficacy of this truth would depend on the extent to which the ego is liberated not from the unconscious alone but from the actual bond to the mother. All too often the causal use of the past offers the patient the opportunity to justify his neurotic symptom or character structure in terms of his history and causes him to remain bound to his mother, insufficiently differentiated—unborn. The therapist, too, may be unaware that the exclusive dependence on making conscious the dynamics of the historic past as therapeutic agent may leave the crucial issue untouched: the crucial issue being the fact that the ego of the patient may be so bound to the mother that he is unable to make constructive use of his knowledge of the past. Rank's contribution lies in his awareness of the possible misuses of the past. He realized that the issue of the patient's bond to the mother was re-created in the actual situation of the analysis, and he was able to make use of it by so constituting the therapeutic situation that it became an opportunity for the patient to live through and experience the process of differentiation.

In his final remarks on psychotherapy Rank reiterates his view that therapy is a *living* process of personality development. His emphasis is on self-autonomy, self-realization, and responsibility as these are developed in the individual by liberating his ability to will without excessive guilt feeling. "The more potentialities the individual has for developing a strong personality of his own, the more forcefully will he express it in new and different forms, given the opportunity. . . . I conceive of human help for the individual not as a planned method of psychotherapeutic techniques but as his experiencing of the irrational forces within himself which he has not heretofore dared to express spontaneously."[22] The ability to provide this helpful opportunity for the patient's growth resides in the therapist's capacity to affirm and accept his emotional life as an expression of his unique, individuated will, and to convey a belief in the realization of his potentialities. In a beautiful passage, Weigert expresses a similar philosophy of therapy: "It is the goal of psychotherapy to reestablish with the patient the bond of solidarity and mutuality in the sense of Antigone's words: 'Not to hate with you, but to love with you am I here.' "[23]

ELEVEN

Rank and Contemporary Social and Psychoanalytic Thought

RANK'S profound philosophical intuition about the totality of human life, about man's dilemma over living with the consciousness of his mortality supersedes his psychology and his therapy. That intuition makes him, a man of our time—perhaps of all time. As the title of his last, posthumously published book, *Beyond Psychology*, suggests, he enlarged the framework of his concerns to include the very nature of *being*—psychologically within its social setting and in relationship to its cosmic dimension. This existential view placed the most basic issue—that of man's awareness of his finiteness—at the heart of the human task of adaptation.

In the current social climate, the task of adapting to the mortality–immortality issue is particularly difficult, since the social institutions which have given structure and meaning to human life are either disappearing or are in a state of flux. Religious conviction, which formerly provided some security for man's need for immortality, has all but gone on this level of belief. In this transitional phase of social evolution, before the emergence of a new and perhaps more abstract level of belief, man is left bereft of meaningfulness. Nor do the secular institutions of society provide him with meaningfulness, especially during crises which threaten his economic security, thereby robbing him not only of the advantages of material affluence and the accompanying satisfaction of work, but also of the illusion that the fulfillment of material wishes beyond the level of actual need for survival could provide meaning in terms of perpetuity. Yet man cannot live without attributing some meaningfulness to his life. He strives ceaselessly to fill a void which appears at certain times in human history when society fails to provide the meaningfulness. This ceaseless search for values to govern not only interaction with others but also to ensure the continuity of human life and thus, through identification, perpetuate the individual life as well, is an aspect of human evolution. Rank as the psychologist and philosopher of progressive evolution was aware of this. And modern biologists are not unmindful of this dimension in human evolution.[1]

Ours is a time of social transition, in which traditional ideologies have lost their meaning, and new ones have either not yet been created or have already been shelved in a mood of disillusionment. In this state of partial alienation individuals turn to a concern with the self—a concern which is reflected in the changed focus of psychological studies. "Modern man became psychological because he became isolated from protective collective ideologies. He had to justify himself from within himself."[2]

In psychoanalytic investigation, from an emphasis on the primacy of life of the instincts and their influence on the structure of personality, there has occurred a shift to an interest in the self, its genesis in interpersonal interaction, its normal characteristics, its malformation, and its reconstruction in the therapeutic situation.

This burgeoning concern with the self has been described by some psychologists and psychoanalysts as a narcissistic regression—a term which has not yet been fully liberated from pejorative implications. Even the term "anthropocentrism" which is used by biologists "is a pejorative in many of the articles which deal with so-called 'ecological crisis.'"[3] So profoundly have our mentors through the ages inveighed against "selfishness," that even in an attempt to understand psychosocial processes, we find it hard to accept their real nature without making a value judgment.

By extending the frames of reference in which he viewed human psychology to include the totality of sociopsychological forces interacting with the constantly changing demands of the environment, Rank transcended the application of values to particular manifestations of human development and behavior. And since he was not committed to a theory of determinism, he was not inclined to turn causality into blame, and thus place the responsibility for changes in individual psychology or in social attitudes at the feet of particular historical events. He accepted a certain randomness in the human life process which he referred to as the existence and operation of irrational forces. For Rank, then, a turning toward the self as a social phenomenon is not a narcissistic regression to be rationally explained, condemned, or overcome. It is simply one aspect of the oscillation in human life between "the two dynamic forces inherent in this human conflict of the individual striving against the social impact of the civilization into which he happens to be born."[4] The duality between self-realization and self-submergence is everpresent and is "a force of balance and not only. . . . a source of conflict."[5] Both are ways in which the individual seeks to ensure immortality: in the case of self-realization through creation, understood in its broadest aspects; in the case of self-submergence through identification with some social, political, or religious ideology (cf. chapter 8). Rank saw beyond the negative implication of a concern with self, and valued it as a positive manifestation of the sociopsychology of the evolutionary life process. While his vision was broader than a clinical understanding of the self and its genesis, it had a profound effect on his clinical practice. For the self-aware creature that was man, the fear of loss of self, and its obverse, the wish for perpetuity, could best be met by the creative fulfillment of the self. Becker, who understood Rank profoundly, sums up Rank's solution for the human dilemma as follows: "some kind of objective creativity is the only answer man has to the problems of life."[6] It is the neurotic who is inhibited in his creative expression and so it is the task of therapy to help him to fulfill his potential for such expressiveness by addressing his fear of separateness and of his individuated self.

It is somewhat ironic that the deepest understanding and appreciation of Rank comes not from a psychologist or a psychoanalyst, but from a scholar in the fields of sociology and political science. Perhaps it took someone outside the psychological field to see the dead end to which the "causal psychologizing" of modern scientific psychology about human happiness and adjustment would eventually lead. It is Becker's existentialism, which he shares with Rank, that enables him to see beyond the value of human rational understanding to its limitations.

Rational understanding of the self is the promise that psychology, as all modern science, held out as the way to happiness; and psychoanalysis proposed to implement understanding in helping the neurotic individual to overcome conflict. As Becker puts it:

> The inner life of man had always been portrayed traditionally as the area of the soul. But in the 19th century scientists wanted to reclaim this last domain of superstition from the Church. They wanted to make the inner life of man an area free of mystery and subject to the laws of causality. They gradually abandoned the word "soul" and began to talk about the "self" and to study how it develops in the child's early relationship with the mother. The great miracles of language, thought and morality could now be studied as social products and not divine interventions. It was a great breakthrough in science that culminated only with the work of Freud; but it was Rank who saw that this scientific victory raised more problems than it solved.[7]

Self-scrutiny and knowledge of the self can only answer man's bad feelings about himself and his social maladaptations *in part*. Knowledge cannot provide meaningfulness. Meaningfulness can only be generated through the individual's own creative efforts or through his identification with a communal ideology. Thus Rank's therapy had to be geared not solely to the acquisition of self knowledge but also to the liberation of the individual will in finding and creating meaning (cf. chapter 10). This affirmation of the indivudal's will by the therapist basically is possible only within the framework of the affirmation of and faith in life itself— in other words, in the context of a fundamentally optimistic view of life. It is at this point that Rank's philosophy of life touches his philosophy of therapy.

Commenting on Rank's life (about which relatively little is known) and attempting to correlate it with his theoretical work, Stolorow and Lachmann have enlarged the significance of his death anxiety as expressed in his adolescent "Day Book" to a life-long "danger of self-fragmentation and self-dissolution—both signaled and concretized by an acute and preoccupying terror of death."[8] Stolorow, writing with G. E. Atwood, has also mistaken an existential awareness of the dimension of mortality in human psychology, as it has been built into Rank's understanding of the human dilemma, for a morbid preoccupation with death.[9] The subjective origin of Rank's theories, as of all theories (a point which Rank himself emphasized), is confirmed not in the danger of his self-fragmentation, but in his creative ability to transcend his personal anxiety and disillusionment by building it into a socially useful theory and therapy.

In the preface to his final work Rank writes, "This book is an attempt to picture human life, not only as I have studied it in many forms for more than a generation, *but as I have achieved it for myself*, in experience, beyond the compulsion to change it in accordance with any man-made ideology."[10] He makes it quite clear that it is his own experience of the acceptance of the nature of life which he has to offer to others so that they, too, through identification, may be enabled to accept the pain of life. For, says Rank, "I have no panacea to offer nor any solution to our human problems which seem to me to be part of man's life on this earth. We are born in pain, we die in pain and we should accept life-pain as unavoidable—indeed a necessary part of earthly existence, not merely the price we have to pay for pleasure."[11]

It is the creation of meaningfulness that reduces the pain of life which is primarily caused by the conscious awareness of mortality. Meaningfulness develops privately for a creative individual, but also, and most importantly for the great majority of people, as the communal ideology of a given historical epoch with which individuals can identify. Becker expresses Rank's critique of psychology in relation to this issue very succinctly when he writes: "psychology has limited its understanding of human unhappiness to the personal life-history of the individual and has not understood how much individual unhappiness is itself a historical problem in the larger sense, a problem of the eclipse of secure communal ideologies of redemption."[12] The *eclipse* of ideologies upon which individuals depend for a sense of meaning in life is the result of cultural, (social, economic, and scientific) development, their *creation* meets man's need for illusion.

Rank was very clear about man's need for illusion, for the historical succession of man-made ideologies[13] are only *believed* to represent truth at a given time, yet it is precisely belief, that is, illusion, that comforts and consoles us, giving us a meaningful place in the cosmic scheme of things. "With the truth one cannot live. To be able to live one needs illusions, not only outer illusions such as art, religion, philosophy, science and love afford, but inner illusions which first condition the outer [i.e., a secure sense of one's active powers, and of being able to count on the powers of others]. The more a man can take reality as truth, appearance as essence, the sounder, the better adjusted, the happier will he be"[14] This is not a cynical plea for falseness or self-deception but an awareness that, as Becker puts it, "man needs a 'second' world, a world of humanly created meaning, a new reality that he can live, dramatize, nourish himself in. 'Illusion' means creative play at its highest level."[15]

To be able to find significance, importance, and pleasure in the limited daily world of human reality is precisely what the neurotic *cannot* do. He does not trust the human-created world of ideologies and meanings and fears, according to Becker, "that human life may not be more than a meaningless interlude in a vicious drama of flesh and bones that we call evolution; that the Creator may not care any more for the destiny of man or the self-perpetuation of individual men than He seems to have cared for the dinosaurs or the Tasmanians. . . . The neurotic is having trouble with the balance of cultural illusion and natural reality."[16]

In more classic psychoanalytic terms one would define this aspect of neurosis either as depression or as failure in the synthesizing of a cohesive self. And indeed when Rank speaks of inner illusions—a secure sense of one's own powers, an ability to count on the powers of others—he is referring to developmental issues which, for the neurotic, have gone awry. They have miscarried because the emotional ambiance and interactions of the childhood situation made it impossible for the individual to effectively separate from the mother and achieve autonomy. But the therapeutic correction of this psychological situation cannot depend exclusively on the acquisition of insight. In Jack Jones' words, "As Rank began to affirm that knowledge was not fundamentally curative, he came to see that the application of psychoanalysis itself was equivocal. Fundamentally it was illusion that cured."[17]

The rational attempts of psychoanalysis aggravated the already exaggerated self-consciousness of the neurotic individual, thus further inhibiting his acceptance of his own human nature and the very nature of life itself. What was curative was the therapist's full acceptance of the human dilemma and therefore of the patient—an acceptance which was probably missing in the course of the person's childhood development. In this sense Rankian treatment offers a corrective experience within the reality of a new situation (cf. chapter 10).

In recent years some psychoanalysts, who originally took a classic psychoanalytic position, have been struck by limitations in the psychoanalytic method and have modified their technical as well as theoretical approach accordingly. Notable among them is Heinz Kohut. His most recent work, *The Restoration of the Self*, suggests a possible relationship to Rank's views, first because of its emphasis on the genesis of the self in interaction with significant others, especially the mother, in the individual's childhood world; and, second, because in his understanding of the therapeutic situation he stresses the importance of correcting the developmental deficit that the patient has suffered through the *reality* of the patient–therapist relationship. While it is true that Kohut claims his technical modifications primarily for the narcissistic personality disorders, his creation of a self psychology addresses itself to a phase of normal personality development and is in many respects reminiscent of Rank. Kohut challenges the primacy of Freudian libido theory as an explanation for the inner life of man: "from the beginning the drive experience is subordinated to the child's experience of the relation between the self and the self-objects."[18] This changes the concept of the centrality of libido theory, and consequently of psychopathology as well.

Rank's insights into human psychological development are quite similar, although some of his terminology belongs to an earlier period in psychoanalytic history. He speaks of "ego" and "object," but, like Kohut, emphasizes the mother relationship not in the anaclitic terms of libido theory but as the original agent of the world of reality. Rank writes,

the mother is for the infant not only the object for the satisfaction of biological needs, but at the same time a representative of the limitations and deprivations stemming from the outer world of reality; in other words, of the 'social' factor in a primitive sense, . . . originally the mother is perceived less as a separate object than as a part of one's own ego. . . . The structuring of ego takes place under the influence of the mother in the pre-oedipal phase and what we refer to psychologically as "Ego" is only a secondary precipitate of the original relationship to the mother.[19]

The fate of the ego depends heavily on the nature of the mother and on her behavior, and in fact influences the child's secondary identification with the father figure. Rank is quite clear that the mechanism of identification takes over and leads to ego building once some separation from the narcissistic tie to the mother has taken place. In the case of positive identification—that is, a loving identification—the ego searches out and finds in the other individual one's own idealized and admired ego (Kohut's grandiose self), while in negative identification the hated and disparaged part of oneself is perceived in the other. In either case, identification both builds the self and represents the possibility of again uniting with and losing oneself in the mother.[20]

The mechanism by which we perceive ourselves in the other is analogous to the mirroring phenomenon described by Kohut. For him, too, the qualitative nature of what is mirrored by the mother, whether love, hate, indifference—determines the nature of the individual's self-feeling. Kohut makes his departure from libido theory quite clear when, in defining oral clinging behavior in relation to the therapist, he states that it is not merely a defense against confrontation with the oedipal conflict (Franz Alexander) but the expression of the needs of an archaic state—needs to which the therapist must be empathically attuned. The attempts to explain such needs solely, in terms of drive, as oral fixation becomes a pejorative judgment and is experienced by the patient as an exhortation to grow up.[21]

"My clinical experience with patients whose severe personality distortions I would formerly have attributed to a fixation of the drive organization at an early level of development (orality), and to the concomitant chronic infantilism of their ego," writes Kohut, "has increasingly taught me that the drive fixation and the widespread ego defects are neither genetically the primary nor dynamic-structurally the most centrally located focus of the psychopathology. It is the self of the child that, in consequence of the *severely disturbed empathic responses of the parents* has not been securely established."[22] In the course of child-rearing, a mother does not only respond to the drives but to a growing self which needs and seeks confirmation for its active, creative, productive expression (Rank's creative will) from the mirroring self-object (the mother). The mother's failure to respond positively to the child's "creative-productive initiative" leads eventually, if this represents a consistently unempathic attitude, to a fragmentation of the child's self.[23] Rank would term this an inhibition in the positive assertive function of the will and he would see its genesis in the same failure of the mother to accept the child's total personality.

For both Rank and Kohut the self, and especially the feeling about the self, is formed through the internalization of experience with the most significant individuals in one's early life. Rank describes this as identification, Kohut as transmuting internalization. In an environment which is traumatically unempathic, the internalizations are of a negative character and result in deficits and fragmentations in the structure of the self and thus in neurotic symptoms and personality disorders. In the opinion of both men, intellectual insight alone, achieved in the course of analysis, cannot correct or heal this faulty development. Kohut says: "the beneficial structural transformations occurring in a successful analysis do not take place as the result of insights. . . .It is not the interpretation that cures the patient."[24]

We have already described Rank's view that knowledge itself is not curative. Therefore, both men in their therapeutic philosophy look to the establishment of an empathic relationship between therapist and patient to make good and repair the patient's early damaged self. In Kohut's view the patient uses the analyst as a new edition of the self-object on which to build the self. Rank speaks of the therapist's acceptance of the patient in his totality as the factor which restores his confidence and self-esteem, thus liberating his will to action.

Interestingly, while both Rank and Kohut are aware of the limitations of libido theory and of a purely intellectual and causal approach in the therapeutic situation, they have arrived at their modifications of psychoanalytic theory and technique along entirely different pathways. Rank's ultimate position represents a complete departure from psychoanalysis; Kohut emphasizes the necessity of giving the patient the opportunity to restore his damaged self by offering oneself as an object for new internalizations. The empathic therapist will support the patient's self-esteem first through affirmation, then by permitting the idealization of his own person so that damage to the self resulting from rejection and disillusionment may be made good. These transitory procedures are needed until the self-structures are solid and autonomous enough to stand on their own. It is clear that Kohut's point of departure is the individual life history. He is concerned with the deficits which the individual has suffered in the course of his development, and with helping him either to overcome them or to compensate for them. To this end he is affirming and empathic.

Rank's *acceptance* of the patient comes not specifically from knowledge of his individual history—although he might be sympathetic to the patient within this framework, too—but from the simple fact of his humanness. For he understood that the depth of human suffering comes from the consciousness of mortality and the need to find meaning in life in the face of the awareness of its transitory and ephemeral nature. So that after the self has been restored and the childhood damage repaired through a new experience, the individual must still accept the nature of life itself and find a creative way to achieve some measure of immortality. It is this broad existential framework which characterizes Rank's thinking and limits the possibility of comparison with other psychological thinkers even when there are similarities in either therapeutic approach or in the focus of concern.

Nevertheless, Rank's work has touched so many aspects of human experience in such a profound way that the echoes of his thought resound in the work of others even without their awareness. One such thinker is Erik Erikson. It is interesting to note that both he and Rank have a background in anthropology; it is therefore not surprising that for both men the perception of the influence of social and cultural factors is central to their view of the development of personality. But again, as with Kohut, Rank, especially in his later works, approaches human problems, however unselfconsciously, from a philosophically existential viewpoint. While Erikson, whose approach to human psychology is developmental, understands the factor of the social milieu as an important determinant in the formation of identity, Rank emphasizes the function of culture as providing those ideological "belief" supports which lend meaning to life and with which an individual can identify in his effort to master the fear of individual mortality.

Rank is keenly aware of the reciprocal relationship between the sociocultural and the individual dimensions in human life. For it is not simply that an individual is born into a specific cultural background at a given time and place, and that his successful adaptation to it determines the synthesis of his identity, nor even that his inborn potentialities for adaptation unfold and are set in motion in specific ways by the historical moment of his existence; it is the *creative* dimension as it is present in certain (heroic) individuals which effects social change—change which in turn influences the lives of all individuals by affecting the nature of their identity formation.[25] Thus the process of psychosocial evolution is in constant flux, with either the influence of the individual or that of society predominating.

From the standpoint of the development of the individual, Erikson defines *personal identity* as "the immediate perception of one's self awareness and continuity in time, and the simultaneous perception of the fact that others recognize one's sameness and continuity."[26] This continuity in identity is, according to Erikson, threatened by historical change. For it was initially the historical (i.e., social) situation from which the individual derived the values and ideals which played a major role in creating his personal identity and giving him a sense of self-esteem and of belonging. Thus the individual is strained in the adaptational task during periods of social transition. Erikson saw this issue, and I believe his observation to be correct, because his focus was on individual disturbance or pathology resulting from interaction with societal change.

But Erikson was also aware that the exceptional individual was able to influence social change by meshing the distinctive character of his own identity formation with the needs and opportunities of a historical moment. His studies of Luther and of Gandhi illustrate this point.[27] Rank, studying the creative products of human history, especially mythology, on the one hand, and focusing on the issue of separation from the parental matrix on the other, wrote: "The detachment of the growing individual from the authority of the parents is one of the most necessary, but also one of the most painful achievements of evolution. It is absolutely necessary for this detachment to take place, and it may be assumed that all normal grown individuals have accomplished it to a certain extent. *Social progress is essentially based upon this opposition between the two generations.*"[28]

For Rank, the hero, as he appears for all peoples throughout the history of world mythology, consistently expresses the exceptional individual's ability to forge an identity that separates him from his origins, yet is appropriate for the historical moment. He embodies the growing ideals and values of a society that will influence its future.

While we owe to Erikson the understanding of the formation of personal identity through the interaction of the individual life history with the societal framework, we must credit Rank, who used a larger historical canvas, with profound insight into the origins of our Western concept of personality. It is a concept which we use loosely and which we generally take for granted. However, "personality" as such did not always exist in human history, and Rank posits its derivation from the emergence and development of Christianity.[29] The disintegration of the Old World of antiquity inaugurated a new spiritual mass movement, namely, Christianity. In its wake there followed a "new philosophy of living . . . and a new psychological type of man," and the idea of a "self" was born. The historical era into which Jesus appeared was, among the Jews, imbued with Messianic ideology. The hoped-for salvation or deliverance from earthly suffering was to come upon the arrival of the Messiah: i.e., from an external event.

According to Rank, Paul was the actual propagator of the Christian movement. He was able, because of his own conversion to spiritualize

> the magic participation of the commoner, the average man. Thus the exceptional type, the deviate who through his own personal conversion was "twice-born" and thereby acquired a new self, became the prototype for the average man, in fact, for mankind. Paul taught that anyone who can believe in Christ—that is, the resurrected Jesus—will himself be resurrected, that is, have a new life, a new *self*, such as he himself had acquired. . . . His was a new kind of living immortality achieved in the creation of personality.[30]

The fundamental human need for an ideology of immortality was met not through psychological identification alone, but through real identity. By virtue of the fact that Paul lives Jesus' life as he himself might have lived it, he *succeeds* him spiritually, becomes as it were his spiritual twin. For Rank the solution of the immortality problem is intimately connected with the issue of succession, for one is immortalized through one's successors. However, in the case of complete identity with another individual, Rank notes, one might speak of self-succession:

> In the history of mankind, we encounter three solutions for the vital problem of succession which developed from the individual desire for immortality into the community problem of preserving the qualities of the fittest. These three solutions—the magical, intellectual and biological—correspond to

three types of civilization, namely, the primitive with its magical succession in The Double, the Greek with its intellectual succession in the disciple, and the Roman with its legalized biological succession in the son. In combining all these conceptions, Christianity reaches beyond them in conceiving of the father—who is biologically denied—as representing the son's own future, whereby a "choice-father" replaces those former relationships. Thus the ancient concepts of re-birth and resurrection were welded into the personality type of self-succession. The prototype of our own "psychological" concept of personality was thereby created.[31]

Both Erikson's conception of "identity" and Rank's of "personality" are different aspects of the life of the self. They are in no way in opposition, but represent differing perspectives and levels of concern. The child who becomes aware that "I am he who can walk"[32] later becomes the man who learns that "I am he who can, by identification with a lasting ideal, achieve a measure of immortality through a creative act of self-formation and change." Both thinkers address themselves to the issue of self-conception, that is to the subjective experience of one's identity; both are aware of the influence of a historical period on the emergence of new identities and both realize the role of the exceptional or deviant personality in implementing the "historical moment" to bring about social change. In his appreciation of Paul's role as the propagator of Christianity through the meshing of his own experience with the historical-social needs of the time, Rank is truly the progenitor of Erikson (in his work on Gandhi and Luther).

In the current atmosphere of psychological focus on the self, the words separation and individuation ring in our ears, and since Rank was concerned with the emergence of the self, initially from the maternal matrix, it is important to compare his thought with those who use a similar terminology. An important figure among them is Margaret Mahler. Are the similarities between Rank and Mahler merely those of terminology, and how deep do the differences go? As we have seen in chapter 6, early in his psychological work Rank was concerned with separation—indeed with the very first separation: birth. But while his main motive at that time, which was the time of the publication of *The Trauma of Birth*, was an attempt to find a paradigm for anxiety, he was already aware of the possibility of psychological birth as it pertained to therapy which offered a "rebirth experience."[33] Significantly, the first chapter of *Truth and*

Reality (1928) is entitled "The Birth of Individuality." Here Rank's view of birth was broadened so far beyond the actual biological experience as to encompass individuation as a psychological process that extends throughout life and is expressed on many levels: "from the birth of the child from the mother, beyond the birth of the individual from the mass, to the birth of the creative work from the individual and finally to the birth of knowledge from the work."[34] The entire process is fueled by the energy of the will, which is an expression of the life force.

It is precisely in relation to the basic conception of the propelling force for human development that Rank differs from those thinkers and observers like Mahler who have remained within the framework of libido theory. The similarity in terminology, separation–individuation, could lead one to assume that they both posit a similar driving force in the formation of an autonomous self. Such is not entirely the case, although there are points of overlap.

It is important to note that Mahler's work is empirical, based on detailed and refined observations of very young children over time. The processes of psychological separation from the mother as well as those of the formation of identity could thus be studied and interpreted in all their varying developmental nuances and phases. It is inevitable, however, that interpretation is colored by the framework of the hypotheses to which the observer is committed. Although Mahler is observing an interaction between mother and child in an effort to show the growth from narcissism to object relationship, the focus of her interpretation is almost exclusively on the child's libidinal development, much as Freud's interpretation of Oedipal impulses is focused on the development of the psychosexual phases of the child's life. For example, while acknowledging the existence of inborn reflexes (sucking, rooting, grasping), Mahler attributes "the baby's turning his head toward the breast in order to achieve the wished-for pleasure he had experienced in previous encounters with the breast" to "pleasure motivation" on the basis of the pleasurable memory of previous encounters.[35] Development is thus viewed as propelled initially and importantly by the pleasure principle, and the archaic awareness of outer reality occurs under the aegis of the pleasure drive (reduction of tension) rather than through the simple developmental unfolding of an innate preceptual process in the service of survival.[36]

Yet there are statements in Mahler's work which seem paradoxical to her emphasis on libido theory and which approximate Rank's thinking about separation anxiety and the emergence of the individual. In speaking of "the strong impetus which drives toward separation," she qualifies this remark in an important footnote: "We know now that the drive is not toward separation per se, but the *innate given is the drive toward individuation*, which cannot be achieved without autonomous separation."[37] The separation–individuation process reverberates throughout the life cycle of the individual (See chapter 4 for Rank's view). Rank, also focusing on the entire life cycle, sees the human developmental process as a conflictful oscillation between a movement toward differentiated autonomy as it expresses itself through the will on the one hand and toward a merging with "the Other," be it individual or ideal, out of the fear of separation on the other hand.

There are other developmental studies of the mother–child interaction, in which the emphasis is less on the issue of individuation than on the emergence of relatedness itself. Since Rank was keenly aware of the social dimension in shaping human life, be it in the early love-feelings between mother and child, or in the influence of larger social forces on the formation of personality, these studies in their social emphasis bear a relationship to his thinking. David Schecter gives us an excellent overview of the work of those investigators whose observations are not confined to the framework of libido theory.[38] In the theories of the Balints, Suttie, Fairbairn, and Bowlby, a primary object-seeking tendency in the infant is posited from the time of birth. Whether indeed it is innate is not as relevant as the fact that this point of view challenges the "orally dominated" Freudian model of the first relatedness. As Erikson and Sullivan point out, "sucking and feeding activities are embedded in a complex relationship between infant and mother, involving subtle mutual adaptations to signs and signals going far beyond oral drive and oral zone per se. The evidence points to the conclusion that the nature of the infant's bond to his mother cannot be reduced to the vicissitudes of oral drive and experience, as important as these must be."[39] The "signs and signals" which pass between mother and infant provide the "social stimulation and reciprocal interaction," which "constitute a basis for the development of specific social attachments between the infant and others."[40] This early development is the precursor of all human communications.

Rank would not be in disagreement with this understanding of the emergence of human relatedness, but in addition, because of his emphasis on the expression of individual identity through the will, he perceived the inevitable social conflict between the will of the self, and the will of "the Other" as it originated in the maternal matrix. It is in this earliest conflict that Rank saw the origins of guilt feeling (Cf chapter 5).

In Rank's time there were no research studies of the kind which Mahler, Escalona, and others undertook. Interpretations were deduced either from clinical observation of pathological states, or, in addition—as in Rank's case—from a knowledge of the products of civilization: mythology, art, religion, history. The scope, therefore, of developmental research studies and Rank's work is vastly different: the former, while sharing some common terminology, observes and interprets the very inception and early development of identity formation, the latter ranges widely over the entire lifetime of an individual, viewing the development of identity as a continuous process throughout life, a process intimately influenced by and interacting with the social setting in which the individual is embedded. Yet Rank was a pioneer in bringing the focus of human development to the mother–child relationship, thereby challenging the primacy of the Oedipus complex in the Freudian schema as the crucial point of development and the nodal point for the development of neurosis. In his clinical work he perceived the enormous psychological difficulty which the individual encounters in the process of separation from the mother and in all the subsequent separations throughout life for which the first separation is the paradigm. He translated this awareness into a profound philosophical understanding of the human need for belonging—that is, uniting with something or someone larger than the self—or of creating something which transcends the self in order to ensure the perpetuity of that self.

It would be unproductive here to draw analogies with the many other depth-psychological thinkers who grew restive under the limitations of Freud's drive theory and shifted the emphasis of their views to a concern with the self in its social dimension.[41] Nevertheless, in Rank's focus on the emergence, the creative expression, and the perpetuation of the self as the subject of psychosocial investigation, he evinces an important relationship to contemporary thought. Yet, because he ranged so broadly over all the manifestations of human psychological life, a comparison with investigators who were bound by specific theories or who confined their observations developmentally to the individual life history, or to derivatives of therapeutic intervention, is inevitably limited and difficult.

From any area of his psychological observation Rank derives some fundamental and generalized life principle. For example, in discussing the issue of separation in the therapeutic situation, he writes "analytic separation becomes the symbol of *separation in general*, which is one of the fundamental life principles. All organic evolution itself rests upon separation, but only the conscious knowledge of this principle on the part of man . . . gives to the concept and the feeling of separation the fundamental psychic meaning." Rank saw the relationship of the "specific psychological" to the "general philosophical." Thus he is unique among psychologists in his overriding philosophical interpretation of the human condition.

Epilogue

As I was approaching the end of my writings about Rank I happened to re-read Earl G. Witenberg's succinct and informative overview of the developments and changes psychoanalysis has undergone within the last 25 years as they are reflected in the essays of the individual authors who had contributed to his volume. It is astounding how much of what has evolved was anticipated by Rank in terms of general direction, if not in specific terminology. First, his emphasis shifted from the Freudian concern with pathology to a focus on normal development. In his emphasis on the nature of the mother–child relationship as crucial for the formation of an autonomous self, he heralded the modern developmental psychologists. Since he was not committed to a deterministic philosophy, Rank saw personality not as fixed by the stamp of the influences of the past, but as a continuously evolving process open to change and choice by virtue of its creative potential. As Witenberg puts it so well: "Man is an act, not a fact, from birth until death."[1] This is a far cry from the early psychoanalytic view that the cornerstone of personality is laid down by the age of five through the resolution of the Oedipus complex; or that we are lived by the id, rather than that we live and evolve.

Many modern psychologists share Rank's awareness of the influence of sociocultural factors on the development of personality. Early on he saw the dangers of emptiness and alienation, and therefore placed the creation of meaningfulness in the center of our adaptive efforts to cope with the existential facts of life.

It is in the creative use of the will that the emphasis of his therapy differs from that of most psychoanalysts. As we have seen, later in his life he ceased to think of himself as an analyst. Yet it is interesting that his view of the therapeutic process has much in common with the thinking of many current psychoanalysts, especially those with an interpersonal orientation. Rather than regarding the therapeutic procedure as a "technique" to be applied to specific human conflicts and problems— and indeed as suitable only for specific types of pathology—Rank shares with others the view that the uniqueness of each individual calls for a different approach in each case. This does not mean that he does not have a general therapeutic philosophy. In fact, his social philosophy, his broad overview of human history, and his insight into the inevitable dilemma of being human have a profound influence upon his therapeutic approach. But because for him therapy is an evolving process within the context of a relationship rather than a search for the applicability of a specific theory, he was able to approach each individual with maximum flexibility. The main tool of his treatment, therefore, was not interpretation but the nature of the relationship between patient and therapist. Within this framework, Rank's emphasis on the therapist's acceptance of the patient as the vehicle for the patient's own ultimate self-acceptance and self-realization foreshadows the emphasis of some modern psychoanalysts on the maintenance of the patient's self-esteem in rebuilding an already damaged sense of self. For Rank, therapy was a new and living experience in the present. Even in his use of dreams he found it more productive to understand them in the light of the current and actual therapeutic situation than to emphasize their derivation from early childhood conflicts. This does not mean that he failed to acknowledge the unconscious precipitates of childhood experience, but that in focusing on the reflections of those experiences in the reality of the interaction with the therapist as a continuing process, the opportunity as well as responsibility for implementing change in personality was placed within the domain of the patient's functioning ego—that is, his will.

For those who share Rank's views or who find them kindred to their own, it is gratifying to find confirmation of their own thoughts and experiences. Yet it is not in such confirmation that the importance of Rank's thought lies. For, despite attempts to impede the development of divergent views, the long history of ideas progresses inevitably through the interaction of social and individual forces, and many men will arrive at similar conclusions. It is in the blending of psychology and social awareness with an avowed philosophy of life that Rank is unique. The optimistic content of this philosophy which ascribes to individuals the creativity with which to transcend their inevitably tragic fate provides meaningfulness for human life. Rank's own life attests to the power of the creative will, for he succeeded in transcending ostracism and isolation, the painful price for deviation from established ideology, by continuing to develop and express his own ideas. Because of the breadth and richness of his philosophical understanding, which is not circumscribed by the limitations of a specific theory, his ideas are "an eternal spring for growth into new dimensions of thought."[2] One can but wonder what gods had to be appeased, what fears allayed, that so rich a legacy has remained so long entombed.

Notes

1. WHY RANK NOW?

1. From Rank's Daybooks, May 14, 1904. In Jessie Taft, *Otto Rank*, p. 29.

2. Donald W. MacKinnon, "Personality and the Realization of Creative Potential," pp. 273–281.

In a later chapter we shall have a good deal to say regarding this neglect of Rank by psychologists and psychoanalysts. However, it is important to note that in the works of the late sociologist Ernest Becker (*The Denial of Death*, 1973, and *Escape from Evil*, 1975) we find a profound understanding and appreciation of Otto Rank's contribution to a psychology of man.

Since these thoughts were formulated, a budding interest in Rank has made its appearance in the psychoanalytic world (Stolorow and Atwood,: "An Ego-Psychological Analysis of the Work and Life of Otto Rank in the Light of Modern Conceptions of Narcissism," pp. 441–459). The authors reflect an appreciation of Rank's timeliness in terms of current psychoanalytic interests and current terminology; yet, to my mind, precisely because of this point of departure, fail to grasp the unique essence of Rank's central concept and the importance of the language in which it is couched. We shall discuss this more fully when we deal with Rank's relationship to contemporary psychoanalytic thought.

3. Ernest G. Schachtel, *Metamorphosis*, pp. 58–60.

4. Rank, *Psychology and the Soul*, p. 32.

5. *Ibid.*, pp. 30–32.

6. See Ernest Becker, *The Denial of Death*. See also Reinhold Niebuhr, *The Nature and Destiny of Man*, p. 73. With no awareness of Rank, he expresses a similar view very succinctly: "science which is *only* [italics mine] science cannot be scientifically accurate. This is particularly true of *Geisteswissenschaft* [humanities] in contrast to physical science. It is more particularly true of psychology

which deals with a dimension of depth in the human spirit, transcending the scientific method. Every rigorous effort to remain within the confines of pure science reduces psychology to physiology, and physiology to bio-mechanics. The ultimate unity and transcendence of the human ego are indeed beyond pure science. Yet it is a necessary undertaking to inquire into the realities of that region 'beyond.'"

7. Feuer, *Einstein and the Generations of Science*, p. 193.

8. *Ibid*, pp. 195–196.

9. Heisenberg, "Planck's Discovery and the Philosophical Problems of Atomic Physics," p. 22.

10. The Einstein quote is from the introduction (March 1929) to Hugo Bergmann's "The Controversy Over the Law of Causality in Recent Physics." *Vieweg Sammlung* no. 98 (Braunschweig, 1929). It, and Rank's following comments appear in *Psychology and the Soul*, pp. 168–69.

11. *Ibid.*, p. 171.

12. Rank, *Beyond Psychology*, p. 48.

2. FREUD AND RANK

1. As recently as 1962, Paul Bergman, reviewing Jessie Taft's biography of Rank in *Psychiatry* (25 [1]:83–85) in a highly subjective, almost caricatured, statement which nevertheless illustrates the prevailing attitudes of the psychoanalytic movement, wrote: "Except for Freud, others found Rank's irritability, uncommunicativeness, and unwillingness to compromise hard to endure. In short, he was the kind of person who today would probably not even be accepted as a psychoanalytic training candidate. Freud, however, saw in Rank creativity, an amazing capacity for work, deep understanding and loyalty, and he considered Rank's uncompromisingness not a liability, but an asset to the young and embattled 'psychoanalytic movement.'" Yet he ends his review on a highly pejorative note: "When Rank died, he left many voluminous books, all hastily written in a difficult idiosyncratic style, in part unpleasant to read, in part incomprehensible. . . . No province of psychology bears his mark; no Rankian school of psychotherapy exists."

In her review of *Art and Artist*, Anais Nin conveys a profound appreciation for "The relevance and contemporary quality" of Rank's contributions. At the same time she points out that Rank's thought was ahead of his time and that his divergence from orthodoxy was punished by a relentless excommunication which "erased (him) from the history of psychoanalysis and from public evaluation of psychoanalytic movements" (p. 94).

2. J. Taft, *Otto Rank*, p. 5.

3. This fact of growth in an overall sense in no way denies the existence of the phenomenon of regression.

4. Taft, *Otto Rank*, p. 4.

5. *Ibid.*, p. 17.

6. *Der Künstler*, 1925 ed., p. 6.

7. Taft, *Otto Rank*, p. 43.

8. Rank uses the term "artist" in the broadest sense, to include creative individuals in many fields: art, music, literature, philosophy, science.

9. E. and W. Menaker, *Ego in Evolution*, pp. 60–61.

10. Rank, *Truth and Reality*, pp. 209–14. *Will Therapy* and *Truth and Reality*, two separate works, were published in English translation as separate volumes by Knopf in 1936 and then republished in one volume in 1945. In this book, the references to these works will be from the 1945 combined volume. *Will Therapy* consists of vols. 2 and 3 of the *Technik der Psychoanalyse*, but not vol. 1, which is called *Die Analytische Situation*. *Truth and Reality* is part 3 of *Genetic Psychology*.

11. See Janik and Toulmin, *Wittgenstein's Vienna*, pp. 74–77 for an accurate picture of the Vienna of the period.

12. Taft, *Otto Rank*, pp. 41, 32, 43.

13. *Ibid.*, p. 37.

14. Rank, *Der Künstler*, 4th ed., pp. 11 and 12. I have here paraphrased the meaning from the original German.

15. Cf. Heisenberg's Uncertainty Principle in L. Von Bertalanffy, *Problems of Life*, p. 177.

16. Fay B. Karpf, *The Psychology and Psychotherapy of Otto Rank*, p. 15.

17. The polarization, and often the irreconcilability, between the clinical findings of psychoanalysis and its theoretical groundwork—its metapsychology—has been discussed in depth in Yankelovich and Barrett, *Ego and Instinct*.

18. Karpf, p. 7n.

19. Rank, *Will Therapy*, p. 122.

20. *Ibid.*, pp. 122–24.

21. Rank, *Art and Artist*, pp. 37–65.

3. CREATIVITY AS THE CENTRAL CONCEPT IN RANK'S PSYCHOLOGY

1. Rank, *Art and Artist*, p. 38.

2. Langer, *Mind: An Essay on Human Feeling*, p. 310.

3. When Rank uses the term "explain"—for example, he does not wish to "explain" the artist, or one cannot "explain" genius—he means one cannot atomistically reduce our understanding to primary causal terms.

4. Rank, *Art and Artist*, p. 25.

5. C. J. Herrick, *The Evolution of Human Nature*, p. 115.

6. Note here that Rank's emphasis on the positive life force, the creative urge, leads him to posit a *wish* for immortality rather than an instinctual impulse toward death (*Todestrieb—Thanatos*).

7. E. H. Erikson, *Identity and the Life Cycle*, p. 22.

8. E. and W. Menaker, *Ego in Evolution*, p. 72.

9. L. W. Flaccus, *The Spirit and Substance of Art*, pp. 65–66.

10. Langer, speaking of individuation on the biological level, remarks:

"Often, indeed, the very means of individuation [are] chiefly powers of aggression against other individuals" (*Mind*, p. 354).

11. Rank, *Art and Artist*, p. 25.

4. THE WILL

1. Taft, *Otto Rank*, pp. 10, 11.
2. *Ibid.*, p. 24.
3. Menaker, "Masochism: A Defense Reaction of the Ego."
4. Rank, *Will Therapy and Truth and Reality*, p. 44.
5. *Ibid.*
6. E. and W. Menaker, *Ego in Evolution*, p. 79.
7. In *Love and Will* Rollo May, without any seeming awareness of Rank's concept of counter-will as the origin of will, notes that "Indeed, the capacity of the infant of two or three to take a negative stand against his parents is very important as the beginning of human will. . . . But if will remains protest, it stays dependent on that which it is protesting against. Protest is half-developed will" (p. 192).
8. Irvin D. Yalom in *Existential Psychotherapy* (pp. 293–97) credits Rank with a schema for the development of will from negative to postive and finally to the emergence of the creative will.
9. Rank, *Will Therapy and Truth and Reality*, p. 212.
10. *Ibid.*, pp. 211–12.
11. *Ibid.*, p. 72. Italics mine—E. M.
12. E. and W. Menaker, *Ego in Evolution*, pp. 150–54.
13. Brown, *Life Against Death*.
14. Becker, *The Denial of Death*, p. 96.
15. Menaker, "Adjustment and Creation."
16. Dixon, *The Human Situation*, p. 225.
17. *Truth and Reality*, p. 260.

5. GUILT

1. Rank, *Genetischen Psychologie*, p. 107.
2. Rank, "Emotion and Denial," pp. 9–25.
3. Such duality is to be distinguished from ambivalence, which is directed *at* the love-object (mother) as love and hate; whereas the duality of which we speak concerns the position of the self vis-à-vis the love-object within the configuration of the self.
4. Cf. Menaker, "Masochism: A Defense Reaction of the Ego."
5. Rank, *Truth and Reality*, pp. 275, 277.
6. Rank, *Art and Artist*, p. 177.
7. Rank, *Truth and Reality*, p. 276.
8. *Ibid.*, pp. 270–91.
9. *Ibid.*, p. 239.

10. *Ibid.*, p. 237.
11. *Ibid.*, p. 238.
12. *Ibid.*, p. 283.
13. Cf. ch. 3 of this work.

6. THE TRAUMA OF BIRTH REEXAMINED

1. Rank, *The Trauma of Birth.*
2. In 1912, after his break with Jung, Freud organized a secret committee of seven most loyal followers to be responsible for the continuation of the psychoanalytic movement. Rank was the youngest member of that committee.
3. Rank, *Trauma of Birth*, pp. 4, 5.
4. *Ibid.*, p. 5.

However, in his later work, *Truth and Reality*, p. 210, especially in the first chapter, "The Birth of Individuality," Rank emphasizes the creative aspect of the individual's psychological birth: "There [in *The Trauma of Birth*] I compared to the creative drive of the individual as treated in *Der Künstler*, the creation of the individual himself, not merely physically, but also psychically in the sense of the 'rebirth experience,' which I understood psychologically as the actual creative act of the human being. For in this act the psychic ego is born out of the biological corporeal ego and the human being becomes at once creator and creature or actually moves from creature to creator, in the ideal case, creator of himself, his own personality."

5. Langer, *Philosophy in a New Key.*
6. Rank, *Trauma of Birth*, p. 215.
7. *Ibid.*, p. 216.
8. In 1911 Rank wrote a paper entitled "Ein Beitrag zum Narcissmus" (A Contribution to Narcissism), which was originally published in *Jahrbach für psychoanalytische und psychopathologische Forschungen*," 1911, vol. 3, and later became a chapter in his book, *Sexualität und Schuldgefühl* (Sexuality and Guilt). Unfortunately, neither the article nor the book have been translated. However, in Freud's paper "On Narcissism," which was published three years later, he refers to Rank's contribution, citing especially a footnote (p. 5 in *Sexualität*) in which Rank finds confirmation in the work of Sadger for his theory that narcissism, which is expressed in love of one's own ego, is founded on an identification with the mother's original idealization of her child. Thus the narcissist, who has incorporated his mother's narcissistic love of him, is at one and the same time mother and child—the admiring and admired.

The importance of this paper and of its concluding observations has a number of aspects. Historically, it places Rank in the vanguard of those who have been concerned with ego phenomena, especially with narcissism. It points up the high esteem in which Rank has been held by Freud, as well as the utter extinction which he experienced in the literature of psychoanalysis after his break with Freud—much to the detriment of its scientific progress. It makes clear Rank's emphasis on the mother–child relationship in which processes of internalization and of separation-individuation are involved, in the structuring of ego. More than fifty years later, Kohut, in *The Analysis of the Self*, in discussing primary narcissism, expounds a view, expressed, it is true, in terms of Freudian energic theory, akin to Rank's in which through processes of internalization the original experience of narcissistic perfection is maintained by a merging of the grandiose self with an idealized parental image to give rise to a "perfect" self-object. In Rank's paper on narcissism, based on the analysis of the dream of a young girl, he describes a very similar process. Many analysts, some who came soon after Rank, like Melanie Klein and Fairbairn, and other contemporary ones like Kohut, Kernberg, Mahler, laboring today in the vineyard which Rank began to cultivate, are unaware of any debt to him.

9. A modern version of the therapeutic importance of the patient's identification with the analyst (a process against which Freud sternly warns in *The Ego and The Id*) is advanced by Kernberg in relation to the treatment of narcissistic personality disorders. He writes as follows: "A narcissistic identification was an idealized and envied image of the therapist, an image that has become more realistic and toned down as a result of the therapist's partial acceptance and partial interpretation of this idealization, may occur as a consequence of introjection by the patient of this ideal image into his grandiose self, thus producing a more adaptive utilization of this pathological structure in his daily life." *Borderline Conditions and Pathological Narcissism*, p. 337.

10. Rank, *Trauma of Birth*, p. 7.
11. Cf. Ernest Becker's *Denial of Death*, pp. 152, 153.
12. Rank, *Trauma of Birth*, pp. 19–20.
13. *Ibid.*, p. 9 (italics mine—E. M.).

7. ANXIETY

1. E. and W. Menaker, *Ego in Evolution*, p. 146.
2. Cf. M. Mahler, et al., *The Psychological Birth of the Human Infant*.
3. Rank, *Will Therapy*, p. 82.
4. E. Menaker, "Masochism: A Defense Reaction of the Ego."
5. Rank, *Will Therapy*, p. 82.
6. *Ibid.*, p. 124.
7. Rank, *Beyond Psychology*, p. 16.

8. THE SOCIAL DIMENSION

1. Mead, *Continuities in Cultural Evolution*, ch. 9.
2. E. and W. Menaker, *Ego in Evolution*, p. 60.
3. Cf. H. Hartmann, *Psychoanalysis and Moral Values*.
4. E. and W. Menaker, *Ego in Evolution*.
5. Freud, *Civilization and Its Discontents*.
6. Cf. Becker, *The Denial of Death*.

7. Rank, *Psychology and the Soul*, pp. 71–93.
8. Freud, *Future of an Illusion*.
9. Rank, *Art and Artist*, pp. 118–19.
10. *Ibid.*, p. 121.
11. *Ibid.*, p. 122.
12. Rank, *The Myth of the Birth of the Hero*.
13. *Ibid.*, p. 72.
14. *Ibid.*, pp. 67–68.
15. E. Menaker, "On Re-Reading *Beyond Psychology*," p. 70.
16. In Rank, *Beyond Psychology*, p. 235.
17. *Ibid.*, p. 236.

9. THE DOUBLE

1. Rank, *The Double*, trans. Harry J. Tucker, Jr., p. 6.
2. Tucker, Introduction to *The Double*, p. xx. See also Virginia P. Robinson, Abstract and Review of *The Double*.
3. Rank, *The Double*, pp. 34–35.
4. Quoted in *Ibid.*, p. 47.
5. *Ibid.*, p. 48.
6. *Ibid.*
7. *Ibid.*, p. 67.
8. *Ibid.*, p. 83.
9. Rank, "The Double as Immortal Self," in *Beyond Psychology*.
10. *Ibid.*, pp. 92, 93.
11. *Ibid.*, pp. 97–98.
12. *Ibid.*, p. 99.
13. Lasch, *The Culture of Narcissism*, pp. 210–11.
14. "The Double as Immortal Self," pp. 98, 99.

10. PSYCHOTHERAPY

1. Jesse Taft, Preface to Rank, *Will Therapy and Truth and Reality*.
2. See Hartmann, *Ego Psychology*.
3. Rank, *Truth and Reality*, p. 222.
4. *Ibid.*, p. 223.
5. Menaker, *Masochism and the Emergent Ego*, p. 95.
6. Rudolf Ekstein, "The Birth and the First 50 Years of Otto Rank's *The Trauma of Birth*," p. 102.
7. Rank, *Technik der Psychoanalyse*, 1:17–18.
8. *Ibid.*, pp. 24, 25.
9. Ekstein, "Rank's Trauma of Birth," p. 97.
10. Cf. Edith Weigert's *The Courage to Love*, in which she says "it is the therapist's love which cures the patient."
11. Rank, "Emotion and Denial," p. 9.

12. *Ibid.*, p. 11 (italics mine—E. M.).

13. Rank, "The Possibilities of Therapy," p. 31.

14. Heinz Kohut, *Restoration of the Self*, p. 13.

15. Cf. E. Menaker, "Masochism: A Defense Reaction of the Ego," p. 205–20. At the time I wrote this paper I was unaware of the relationship between my concerns with separation and Rank's theories.

16. I originally reported this in *Masochism and the Emergent Ego*, ch. 6, p. 95. It is worth repeating here not only because it illustrates the overwhelming fear of individuation, and the crucial depth of the separation issue in the overcoming of neurosis, but also because the importance of recovered memories in the transference reaction is juxtaposed to the possibility for creative change in the actuality of the current situation. It is the latter upon which Rank places particular emphasis.

17. Rank, *Technik der Psychoanalyse*, pp. 142–51.

18. Gardiner, ed. *The Wolfman*, p. 157.

19. Brunswick, "A Supplement to Freud's History of an Infantile Neurosis."

20. Rank, *Technik der Psychoanalyse*, p. 207.

21. Sandor Ferenczi, "Zur Kritik der Rankschen *Technik der Psychoanalyse.*"

22. Rank, *Beyond Psychology*, pp. 47–51.

23. Weigert, *The Courage To Love*, p. 107.

11. RANK AND CONTEMPORARY THOUGHT

1. See W. H. Murdy, "Anthropocentrism: A Modern Version."

2. Becker, *Denial of Death*, pp. 190–91.

3. Murdy, "Anthropocentrism," p. 116.

4. Rank, *Beyond Psychology*, p. 15.

5. *Ibid.*, p. 21.

6. Becker, *Denial of Death*, p. 185.

7. *Ibid.*, p. 191.

8. Robert D. Stolorow and Frank M. Lachman, *Psychoanalysis of Developmental Arrests*, p. 126.

9. Stolorow and G. E. Atwood, "An Ego-Psychological Analysis of the Work and Life of Otto Rank, in the Light of Modern Conceptions of Narcissism," p. 441.

10. Rank, *Beyond Psychology*, p. 16.

11. *Ibid.*, p. 16.

12. Becker, *Denial of Death*, p. 193.

13. For Rank "ideology" means *Weltanschauung*, or view of life.

14. Rank, *Truth and Reality*, pp. 251–52.

15. Becker, *Denial of Death*, p. 189.

16. *Ibid.*, pp. 187–88.

17. Jack Jones, "Otto Rank: A Forgotten Heresy," pp. 219–29.

18. Kohut, *Restoration of the Self*, p. 80.

19. Rank, *Grundzüge, einer Genetischen Psychologie*, p. 43. My translation—E. M.

20. *Ibid.*, pp. 134–44.

21. Kohut, *Restoration*, p. 70.

22. *Ibid.*, p. 14 (italics mine—E. M.).

23. *Ibid.*, p. 76.

24. *Ibid.*, pp. 30–31.

25. Cf. E. and W. Menaker, *Ego in Evolution*, pp. 55–62.

26. Erikson, "Ego Development and Historical Change," p. 23.

27. Erikson, *Young Man Luther; Gandhi's Truth.*

28. Rank, *The Myth of the Birth of the Hero*, pp. 67–68 (italics mine—E. M.).

29. Rank, *Beyond Psychology*, pp. 144–72.

30. *Ibid.*, p. 159.

31. *Ibid.*, p. 162.

32. Erikson, *Ego Development and Historical Change*, p. 22.

33. Rank, *Truth and Reality*, p. 210.

34. *Ibid.*, p. 220.

35. Mahler, *The Psychological Birth of the Human Infant*, p. 42.

36. Cf. Charlotte Buhler's developmental studies.

37. Mahler, *Psychological Birth*, p. 9 (italics mine—E. M.).

38. Schecter, "On the Emergence of Human Relatedness," pp. 17–39.

39. *Ibid.*, p. 19.

40. *Ibid.*, p. 21.

41. Karen Horney (*Neurosis and Human Growth*) is an excellent example of a psychoanalyst who early on emphasized the constructive growth potential of the self.

EPILOGUE

1. Witenberg, "Psychology Today," pp. 3–11. The quotation is from page 4.

2. Becker, *Denial of Death*, p. 92.

Bibliography

WRITINGS OF OTTO RANK

Art and Artist. New York: Knopf, 1932.

"Ein Beitrag zum Narcissmus." *Jahrbuch für Psychoanalytische und Psychopathologische Forschungen*, (1911), vol. 3.

Beyond Psychology. New York: Dover, 1958. (reprint of original publication, 1941).

The Don Juan Legend. Translated and edited by David G. Winter. Princeton, N.J.: Princeton University Press, 1975.

The Double. Translated and edited by Harry J. Tucker, Jr. Chapel Hill: North Carolina University Press, 1971.

"Emotion and Denial." *Journal of the Otto Rank Association* (1968), 3 (1). (Translated from "Gestaltung und Ausdruck der Persönlichkeit." In Rank, *Genetischen Psychologie q.v.*

Grundzüge einer Genetischen Psychologie. (Genetic Psychology) Vienna: Franz Deuticke, 1927. (Vol. 3 of this work is translated under the title *Truth and Reality*, New York, Knopf 1936 and 1945.)

Der Künstler, 2d ed. Vienna: Internationaler Psychoanalytischer Verlag, 1925. (1st ed.: Vienna: H. Heller, 1907.)

The Myth of the Birth of the Hero. New York: Vintage, 1964.

"The Possibilities of Therapy." *Journal of the Otto Rank Association* (1968) 3 (1). Translated from *Genetischen Psychologie, q.v.*

Psychology and the Soul. New York: A. S. Barnes, Perpetua Edition, 1961.

Sexualität und Schuldgefühl (Sexuality and Guilt). Vienna: Internationaler Psychoanalytischer Verlag, 1926.

Technik der Psychoanalyse 1: Die Analytische Situation. Vienna: Deuticke, 1926. (Vols. 2 and 3 of "Technik" are in English translation under the title *Will Therapy,* N.Y. Knopf, 1936, 1945.)

The Trauma of Birth. New York: Harper &Row (Torchbook ed.), 1973. (Original English translation 1929.)

Truth and Reality. New York: Knopf, 1945.

Will Therapy and Truth and Reality. New York: Knopf, 1945.

OTHER SOURCES

Becker, Ernest. *The Denial of Death.* New York: Free Press, 1973.

Becker, Ernest. *Escape from Evil.* New York: Free Press, 1975.

Bergman, Paul. Book Review. "The Dissident Schools." *Psychiatry* (1962) 25 (1).

Bertalanffy, Ludwig von. *Problems of Life.* New York: Harper & Row, 1960.

Brown, Norman O. *Life Against Death.* New York: Viking, 1959.

Brunswick, Ruth Mack. "A Supplement to Freud's History of an Infantile Neurosis." In Gardiner, ed. *The Wolfman, q.v.*

Bühler, Charlotte. *Kindheit und Jugend.* Leipzig: Verlag von S. Hirzel, 1931.

Comte, Auguste. *Cours de Philosophie Positive.* Paris: 1830. (5th ed., 1892.)

Dixon, W. Macneile. *The Human Situation.* New York: Oxford University Press, 1958.

Ekstein, Rudolf. "The Birth and the First 50 Years of Otto Rank's The Trauma of Birth." *Journal of the Otto Rank Association* (Winter 1973-74) 8 (2).

Erikson, Erik H. "Ego Development and Historical Change," in *Psychological Issues* 1 (1). New York: International Univerersities Press, 1959.

Erikson, Erik H. *Identity and the Life Cycle.* Psychological Issues, 1 (1). Monograph I. New York: International Universities Press, 1959.

Erikson, Erik H. *Gandhi's Truth.* New York: Norton, 1969.

Erikson, Erik H. *Young Man Luther.* New York: Norton, 1962.

Fenichel, Otto. *The Psychoanalytic Theory of Neurosis.* New York: Norton, 1945.

Ferenczi, Sandor. "Zur Kritik der Rankschen *Technik der Psychoanalyse" Int. Zeitschrift für Psychoanalyse* (1924) 13 (1).

Feuer, Lewis S. *Einstein and the Generations of Science.* New York: Basic Books, 1974.

Flaccus, L. W. *The Spirit and Substance of Art.* New York: F. S. Crofts & Co., 1926.

Freud, Sigmund. *Civilization and its Discontents.* New York: Doubleday, 1958.

Freud, Sigmund. "From the History of an Infantile Neurosis." London: Collected Papers, vol. 3, Hogarth Press, 1953. Also in Gardiner, ed *The Wolfman, q.v.*

Freud, Sigmund. *The Future of an Illusion.* Vienna: Int. Psa. Verlag, Gesammelte Werke, 11, Standard Edition 21.

Gardiner, Muriel, ed. *Wolf Man: With The Case of The Wolf Man by Sigmund Freud.* New York: Basic Books, 1971.

Hartmann, Heinz. *Ego Psychology and the Problem of Adaptation.* New York: International Universities Press, 1958.

Hartmann, Heinz. *Psychoanalysis and Moral Values.* New York: International Universities Press, 1960.

Heisenberg, Werner. "Planck's Discovery and the Philosophical Problems of Atomic Physics." In Heisenberg et al., eds. *On Modern Physics.* New York: Clarkson N. Potter, 1961.

Herrick, C. J. *The Evolution of Human Nature.* Austin: University of Texas Press, 1956.

Horney, Karen. *Neurosis and Human Growth.* New York: Norton, 1950.

Janik, Allan and Stephen Toulmin. *Wittgenstein's Vienna.* New York: Simon and Schuster, 1973.

Jones, Jack. "Otto Rank: A Forgotten Heresy." *Commentary*, September 1960.

Karpf, Fay B. *The Psychology and Psychotherapy of Otto Rank.* New York: Philosophical Library, 1953.

Kernberg, Otto. *Borderline Conditions and Pathological Narcissism.* New York: Aronson, 1975.

Kohut, Heinz. *The Analysis of the Self.* New York: International Universities Press, 1971.

Kohut, Heinz. *The Restoration of the Self.* New York: International Universities Press, 1977.

Langer, Susanne K. *Mind: An Essay on Human Feeling.* Baltimore: Johns Hopkins Press, 1967.

Langer, Susanne K. *Philosophy in a New Key.* Cambridge: Harvard University Press, 1942.

Lasch, Christopher. *The Culture of Narcissism.* New York: Norton, 1978.

MacKinnon, Donald W. "Personality and the Realization of Creative Potential." *American Psychologist* (April 1965) 20 (4).

Mahler, Margaret, F. Pine, and A. Bergman. *The Psychological Birth of the Human Infant.* New York: Basic Books, 1975.

May, Rollo. *Love and Will.* New York: Norton, 1969.

Mead, Margaret. *Continuities in Cultural Evolution.* New Haven: Yale University Press, 1964.

Menaker, Esther. "Adjustment and Creation." *Journal of the Otto Rank Association* (June 1972) 7 (1).

Menaker, Esther. "Masochism: A Defense Reaction of the Ego." *Psychoanalytic Quarterly* (1953) 22.

Menaker, Esther. *Masochism and the Emergent Ego.* Selected Papers, ed. Leila Lerner. New York: Human Sciences Press, 1979.

Menaker, Esther. "On Re-reading *Beyond Psychology.*" *Journal of the Otto Rank Association* (June 1968) 3 (1).

Menaker, Esther and William. *Ego in Evolution.* New York: Grove Press, 1965.

Merezhkovsky, Dmitri. From *Tolstoi and Dostojewski* in Tucker translation of Rank, *The Double, q.v.*

Murdy, W. H. "Anthropocentrism: A Modern Version." *Science* March 28, 1975.

Niebuhr, Reinhold. *The Nature and Destiny of Man.* New York: Scribner, 1941.

Nin, Anaïs. "On Truth and Reality." *Journal of the Otto Rank Association* (1973) 8 (1).

Nin, Anaïs. Review of *Art and Artist. Journal of the Otto Rank Association* (December 1968) 3 (2).

Robinson, Virginia P. Abstract and Review of Otto Rank's *The Double. Journal of the Otto Rank Association* (December 1971) 6 (2).

Schachtel, Ernest G. *Metamorphosis.* New York: Basic Books, 1959.

Schecter, David. "On the Emergence of Human Relatedness." In Earl G. Witenberg, ed., *Interpersonal Explorations in Psychoanalysis.* New York: Basic Books, 1973.

Stolorow, Robert D. and George E. Atwood. "An Ego-Psychological Analysis of the Work and Life of Otto Rank in the Light of Modern Conceptions of Narcissism." *The International Review of Psychoanalysis* (1976) 3 (part 4);441–59.

Stolorow, Robert D. and Frank M. Lachman. *Psychoanalysis of Developmental Arrests.* New York: International Universities Press, 1980.

Taft, Jessie. *Otto Rank.* New York: Julian Press, 1958.

Taft, Jessie. Translator's Preface to Rank's *Will Therapy and Truth and Reality, q.v.*

Weigert, Edith. *The Courage to Love.* New Haven: Yale University Press, 1970.

Witenberg, Earl G. "Psychology Today." In Witenberg, ed. *Interpersonal Explorations in Psychoanalysis.* New York: Basic Books, 1973.

Yalom, Irvin D.: *Existential Psychotherapy,* New York, Basic Books, 1980.

Yankelovich, Daniel and William Barrett. *Ego and Instinct.* New York: Random House, 1970.

Index